CAMBRIDGE LIBRARY COLLECTION

Books of enduring scholarly value

English Men of Letters

In the 1870s, Macmillan publishers began to issue a series of books called 'English Men of Letters' – biographies of English writers by other English writers. The general editor of the series was the journalist, critic, politician, and supporter (and later biographer) of Gladstone, John Morley (1838–1923). The first volume published was Samuel Johnson, by Leslie Stephen (1878), and the first series (which continued until 1892) eventually consisted of 39 volumes. The aim was to provide a short introduction to each subject and his works, but also that the life should illuminate the works, and vice versa. All the subjects were men, as were all but one of the authors (Mrs Oliphant on Sheridan); and all but one (Hawthorne) were English or Irish. The subjects range chronologically from Chaucer to Thackeray and Dickens, and an important feature of the series is that many of the authors (Henry James on Hawthorne, Ward on Dickens) were discussing writers of the previous generation, and some (Trollope on Thackeray) had even known their subjects personally. The series exemplifies the British approach to literary biography and criticism at the end of the nineteenth century, and also reveals which authors were at that time regarded as canonical.

Shelley

John Addington Symonds (1840–93), well known as an author, poet and critic, wrote this biography of the poet Percy Bysshe Shelley (1792–1822) in an attempt to portray the complete man. Shelley, Symonds writes, was more than a controversial atheist. He was full of earnest conviction, enthusiasm, and intellectual vigour, but also extravagance, crudity and presumption. Published in 1878 in the first series of English Men of Letters, this book thus provides an account of a literary life famously cut short, describing a writer whose intellectual and poetic legacy was perhaps not fully appreciated in the Victorian period, when the response to his poems was frequently coloured by antipathy to his revolutionary ideas and his unconventional private life, as well as to his loudly proclaimed atheism.

Cambridge University Press has long been a pioneer in the reissuing of out-of-print titles from its own backlist, producing digital reprints of books that are still sought after by scholars and students but could not be reprinted economically using traditional technology. The Cambridge Library Collection extends this activity to a wider range of books which are still of importance to researchers and professionals, either for the source material they contain, or as landmarks in the history of their academic discipline.

Drawing from the world-renowned collections in the Cambridge University Library, and guided by the advice of experts in each subject area, Cambridge University Press is using state-of-the-art scanning machines in its own Printing House to capture the content of each book selected for inclusion. The files are processed to give a consistently clear, crisp image, and the books finished to the high quality standard for which the Press is recognised around the world. The latest print-on-demand technology ensures that the books will remain available indefinitely, and that orders for single or multiple copies can quickly be supplied.

The Cambridge Library Collection will bring back to life books of enduring scholarly value (including out-of-copyright works originally issued by other publishers) across a wide range of disciplines in the humanities and social sciences and in science and technology.

Shelley

JOHN ADDINGTON SYMONDS

CAMBRIDGE
UNIVERSITY PRESS

CAMBRIDGE UNIVERSITY PRESS

Cambridge, New York, Melbourne, Madrid, Cape Town,
Singapore, São Paolo, Delhi, Tokyo, Mexico City

Published in the United States of America by Cambridge University Press, New York

www.cambridge.org
Information on this title: www.cambridge.org/9781108034692

© in this compilation Cambridge University Press 2011

This edition first published 1878
This digitally printed version 2011

ISBN 978-1-108-03469-2 Paperback

English Men of Letters

EDITED BY JOHN MORLEY

SHELLEY

SHELLEY

BY

JOHN ADDINGTON SYMONDS

London:
MACMILLAN AND CO.
1878.

LONDON :
GILBERT AND RIVINGTON, PRINTERS,
ST. JOHN'S SQUARE.

CONTENTS.

LIST OF AUTHORITIES.

1. The Poetical and Prose Works of Percy Bysshe Shelley, edited by Mrs. Shelley. Moxon, 1840, 1845. 1 vol.

2. The Poetical Works, edited by Harry Buxton Forman. Reeves and Turner, 1876–7. 4 vols.

3. The Works of Percy Bysshe Shelley, edited by W. M. Rossetti. Moxon, 1870. 2 vols.

4. Hogg's Life of Shelley. Moxon, 1858. 2 vols.

5. Trelawny's Records of Shelley, Byron, and the Author. Pickering, 1878. 2 vols.

6. Shelley Memorials, edited by Lady Shelley. Smith and Elder. 1 vol.

7. Medwin's Life of Shelley. Newby, 1847. 2 vols.

8. Shelley's Early Life, by D. F. McCarthy. Chatto and Windus. 1 vol.

9. Leigh Hunt's Autobiography. Smith and Elder.

10. W. M. Rossetti's Life of Shelley, included in the edition above cited, No. 3.

11. Shelley, a Critical Biography, by G. B. Smith. David Douglas, 1877.

12. Relics of Shelley, edited by Richard Garnett. Moxon, 1862.

13. Peacock's Articles on Shelley in *Fraser's Magazine*, 1858 and 1860.

14. Shelley in Pall Mall, by R. Garnett, in *Macmillan's Magazine*, June, 1860.

15. Shelley's Last Days, by R. Garnett, in the *Fortnightly Review*, June, 1878.

16. Two Lectures on Shelley, by W. M. Rossetti, in the *University Magazine*, February and March, 1878.

SHELLEY.

CHAPTER I.

BIRTH AND CHILDHOOD.

IT is worse than useless to deplore the irremediable; yet no man, probably, has failed to mourn the fate of mighty poets, whose dawning gave the promise of a glorious day, but who passed from earth while yet the light that shone in them was crescent. That the world should know Marlowe and Giorgione, Raphael and Mozart, only by the products of their early manhood, is indeed a cause for lamentation, when we remember what the long lives of a Bach and Titian, a Michelangelo and Goethe, held in reserve for their maturity and age. It is of no use to persuade ourselves, as some have done, that we possess the best work of men untimely slain. Had Sophocles been cut off in his prime, before the composition of *Œdipus*; had Handel never merged the fame of his forgotten operas in the immortal music of his oratorios; had Milton been known only by the poems of his youth, we might with equal plausibility have laid that flattering unction to our heart. And yet how shallow would have been our optimism, how fallacious our attempt at consolation. There is no denying

B

the fact that when a young Marcellus is shown by fate for
one brief moment, and withdrawn before his spring-time
has brought forth the fruits of summer, we must bow in
silence to the law of waste that rules inscrutably in nature.

Such reflections are forced upon us by the lives of three
great English poets of this century. Byron died when he
was thirty-six, Keats when he was twenty-five, and Shelley
when he was on the point of completing his thirtieth year.
Of the three, Keats enjoyed the briefest space for the
development of his extraordinary powers. His achievement, perfect as it is in some poetic qualities, remains so
immature and incomplete that no conjecture can be
hazarded about his future. Byron lived longer and produced more than his brother poets. Yet he was extinguished when his genius was still ascendant, when his
"swift and fair creations" were issuing like worlds from
an archangel's hands. In his case we have perhaps only to
deplore the loss of masterpieces that might have equalled,
but could scarcely have surpassed, what we possess.
Shelley's early death is more to be regretted. Unlike
Keats and Byron he died by a mere accident. His faculties were far more complex, and his aims were more
ambitious than theirs. He therefore needed length of
years for their co-ordination; and if a fuller life had been
allotted him, we have the certainty that from the discords
of his youth he would have wrought a clear and lucid
harmony.

These sentences form a somewhat gloomy prelude to a
biography. Yet the student of Shelley's life, the sincere
admirer of his genius, is almost forced to strike a solemn
key-note at the outset. We are not concerned with one
whose "little world of man" for good or ill, was perfected,
but with one whose growth was interrupted just before

the synthesis of which his powers were capable, had been accomplished.

August 4, 1792, is one of the most memorable dates in the history of English literature. On this day Percy Bysshe Shelley was born at Field Place, near Horsham, in the county of Sussex. His father, named Timothy, was the eldest son of Bysshe Shelley, Esquire, of Goring Castle, in the same county. The Shelley family could boast of great antiquity and considerable wealth. Without reckoning earlier and semi-legendary honours, it may here be recorded that it is distinguished in the elder branch by one baronetcy dating from 1611, and by a second in the younger dating from 1806. In the latter year the poet's grandfather received this honour through the influence of his friend the Duke of Norfolk. Mr. Timothy Shelley was born in the year 1753, and in 1791 he married Elizabeth, daughter of Charles Pilfold, Esquire, a lady of great beauty, and endowed with fair intellectual ability, though not of a literary temperament. The first child of this marriage was the poet, named Bysshe in compliment to his grandfather, the then living head of the family, and Percy because of some remote connexion with the ducal house of Northumberland. Four daughters, Elizabeth, Mary, Hellen, and Margaret, and one son, John, who died in the year 1866, were the subsequent issue of Mr. Timothy Shelley's marriage. In the year 1815, upon the death of his father, he succeeded to the baronetcy, which passed, after his own death, to his grandson, the present Sir Percy Florence Shelley, as the poet's only surviving son.

Before quitting, once and for all, the arid region of genealogy, it may be worth mentioning that Sir Bysshe Shelley by his second marriage with Miss Elizabeth Jane

Sydney Perry, heiress of Penshurst, became the father of five children, the eldest son of whom assumed the name of Shelley-Sidney, received a baronetcy, and left a son, Philip Charles Sidney, who was created Lord De l'Isle and Dudley. Such details are not without a certain value, inasmuch as they prove that the poet, who won for his ancient and honourable house a fame far more illustrious than titles can confer, was sprung from a man of no small personal force and worldly greatness. Sir Bysshe Shelley owed his position in society, the wealth he accumulated, and the honours he transmitted to two families, wholly and entirely to his own exertions. Though he bore a name already distinguished in the annals of the English landed gentry, he had to make his own fortune under conditions of some difficulty. He was born in North America, and began life, it is said, as a quack doctor. There is also a legend of his having made a first marriage with a person of obscure birth in America. Yet such was the charm of his address, the beauty of his person, the dignity of his bearing, and the vigour of his will, that he succeeded in winning the hands and fortunes of two English heiresses ; and, having begun the world with nothing, he left it at the age of seventy-four, bequeathing 300,000*l.* in the English Funds, together with estates worth 20,000*l.* a year to his descendants.

Percy Bysshe Shelley was therefore born in the purple of the English squirearchy ; but never assuredly did the old tale of the swan hatched with the hen's brood of ducklings receive a more emphatic illustration than in this case. Gifted with the untameable individuality of genius, and bent on piercing to the very truth beneath all shams and fictions woven by society and ancient usage, he was driven by the circumstances of his birth and his surroundings

into an exaggerated warfare with the world's opinion.
His too frequent tirades against—

> The Queen of Slaves,
> The hood-winked Angel of the blind and dead,
> Custom,—

owed much of their asperity to the early influences brought
to bear upon him by relatives who prized their position in
society, their wealth, and the observance of conventional
decencies, above all other things.

Mr. Timothy Shelley was in no sense of the word a
bad man ; but he was everything which the poet's father
ought not to have been. As member for the borough
of Shoreham, he voted blindly with his party ; and that
party looked to nothing beyond the interests of the
gentry and the pleasure of the Duke of Norfolk. His
philosophy was limited to a superficial imitation of
Lord Chesterfield, whose style he pretended to affect in
his familiar correspondence, though his letters show that
he lacked the rudiments alike of logic and of grammar.
His religious opinions might be summed up in Clough's
epigram :—

> At church on Sunday to attend
> Will serve to keep the world your friend.

His morality in like manner was purely conventional,
as may be gathered from his telling his eldest son that he
would never pardon a *mésalliance,* but would provide for
as many illegitimate children as he chose to have. For the
rest, he appears to have been a fairly good landlord, and a
not unkind father, sociable and hospitable, somewhat vain
and occasionally odd in manner, but qualified for passing
muster with the country gentlemen around him. In the
capacity to understand a nature which deviated from the

ordinary type so remarkably as Shelley's, he was utterly
deficient; and perhaps we ought to regard it as his mis-
fortune that fate made him the father of a man who was
among the greatest portents of originality and unconven-
tionality that this century has seen. Toward an ordinary
English youth, ready to sow his wild oats at college, and
willing to settle at the proper age and take his place upon
the bench of magistrates, Sir Timothy Shelley would
have shown himself an indulgent father; and it must be
conceded by the poet's biographer that if Percy Bysshe
had but displayed tact and consideration on his side, many
of the misfortunes which signalized his relations to his
father would have been avoided.

Shelley passed his childhood at Field Place, and when
he was about six years old began to be taught, together
with his sisters, by Mr. Edwards, a clergyman who lived at
Warnham. What is recorded of these early years we owe
to the invaluable communications of his sister Hellen.
The difference of age between her and her brother Bysshe
obliges us to refer her recollections to a somewhat later
period—probably to the holidays he spent away from
Sion House and Eton. Still, since they introduce us to
the domestic life of his then loved home, it may be proper
to make quotations from them in this place. Miss Shelley
tells us that her brother "would frequently come to the
nursery, and was full of a peculiar kind of pranks. One
piece of mischief, for which he was rebuked, was running
a stick through the ceiling of a low passage to find some
new chamber, which could be made effective for some
flights of his vivid imagination." He was very much
attached to his sisters, and used to entertain them with
stories, in which "an alchemist, old and grey, with a
long beard," who was supposed to abide mysteriously in

the garret of Field Place, played a prominent part. "Another favourite theme was the 'Great Tortoise,' that lived in Warnham Pond; and any unwonted noise was accounted for by the presence of this great beast, which was made into the fanciful proportions most adapted to excite awe and wonder." To his friend Hogg, in after-years, Shelley often spoke about another reptile, no mere creature of myth or fable, the "Old Snake," who had inhabited the gardens of Field Place for several generations. This venerable serpent was accidentally killed by the gardener's scythe; but he lived long in the poet's memory, and it may reasonably be conjectured that Shelley's peculiar sympathy for snakes was due to the dim recollection of his childhood's favourite. Some of the games he invented to please his sisters were grotesque, and some both perilous and terrifying. "We dressed ourselves in strange costumes to personate spirits or fiends, and Bysshe would take a fire-stove and fill it with some inflammable liquid and carry it flaming into the kitchen and to the back door." Shelley often took his sisters for long country rambles over hedge and fence, carrying them when the difficulties of the ground or their fatigue required it. At this time "his figure was slight and beautiful,—his hands were models, and his feet are treading the earth again in one of his race; his eyes too have descended in their wild fixed beauty to the same person. As a child, I have heard that his skin was like snow, and bright ringlets covered his head." Here is a little picture which brings the boy vividly before our eyes: "Bysshe ordered clothes according to his own fancy at Eton, and the beautifully fitting silk pantaloons, as he stood as almost all men and boys do, with their coat-tails near the fire, excited my silent though excessive admiration."

When he was ten years of age, Shelley went to school at Sion House, Brentford, an academy kept by Dr. Greenlaw, and frequented by the sons of London tradesmen, who proved but uncongenial companions to his gentle spirit. It is fortunate for posterity that one of his biographers, his second cousin Captain Medwin, was his schoolfellow at Sion House ; for to his recollections we owe some details of great value. Medwin tells us that Shelley learned the classic languages almost by intuition, while he seemed to be spending his time in dreaming, now watching the clouds as they sailed across the school-room window, and now scribbling sketches of fir-trees and cedars in memory of Field Place. At this time he was subject to sleep-walking, and, if we may credit this biographer, he often lost himself in reveries not far removed from trance. His favourite amusement was novel-reading ; and to the many " blue books " from the Minerva press devoured by him in his boyhood, we may ascribe the style and tone of his first compositions. For physical sports he showed no inclination. " He passed among his schoolfellows as a strange and unsocial being ; for when a holiday relieved us from our tasks, and the other boys were engaged in such sports as the narrow limits of our prison-court allowed, Shelley, who entered into none of them, would pace backwards and forwards— I think I see him now—along the southern wall, indulging in various vague and undefined ideas, the chaotic elements, if I may say so, of what afterwards produced so beautiful a world."

Two of Shelley's most important biographical compositions undoubtedly refer to this period of his boyhood. The first is the passage in the Prelude to *Laon and Cythna* which describes his suffering among the unsympathetic inmates of a school—

Thoughts of great deeds were mine, dear Friend, when first
The clouds which wrap this world from youth did pass.
I do remember well the hour which burst
My spirit's sleep : a fresh May-dawn it was,
When I walked forth upon the glittering grass,
And wept, I knew not why ; until there rose
From the near school-room, voices, that, alas !
Were but one echo from a world of woes—
The harsh and grating strife of tyrants and of foes.

And then I clasped my hands and looked around—
—But none was near to mock my streaming eyes,
Which poured their warm drops on the sunny ground—
So without shame I spake :—" I will be wise,
And just, and free, and mild, if in me lies
Such power, for I grow weary to behold
The selfish and the strong still tyrannize
Without reproach or check."   I then controlled
My tears, my heart grew calm, and I was meek and bold.

And from that hour did I with earnest thought
Heap knowledge from forbidden mines of lore,
Yet nothing that my tyrants knew or taught
I cared to learn, but from that secret store
Wrought linkèd armour for my soul, before
It might walk forth to war among mankind.
Thus power and hope were strengthened more and more
Within me, till there came upon my mind
A sense of loneliness, a thirst with which I pined.

The second is a fragment on friendship preserved by
Hogg. After defining that kind of passionate attachment
which often precedes love in fervent natures, he proceeds :
" I remember forming an attachment of this kind at
school. I cannot recall to my memory the precise epoch
at which this took place ; but I imagine it must have
been at the age of eleven or twelve. The object of these
sentiments was a boy about my own age, of a character
eminently generous, brave, and gentle ; and the elements

of human feeling seemed to have been, from his birth, genially compounded within him. There was a delicacy and a simplicity in his manners, inexpressibly attractive. It has never been my fortune to meet with him since my school-boy days; but either I confound my present recollections with the delusions of past feelings, or he is now a source of honour and utility to every one around him. The tones of his voice were so soft and winning, that every word pierced into my heart; and their pathos was so deep, that in listening to him the tears have involuntarily gushed from my eyes. Such was the being for whom I first experienced the sacred sentiments of friendship." How profound was the impression made on his imagination and his feelings by this early friendship, may again be gathered from a passage in his note upon the antique group of Bacchus and Ampelus at Florence. "Look, the figures are walking with a sauntering and idle pace, and talking to each other as they walk, as you may have seen a younger and an elder boy at school, walking in some grassy spot of the play-ground with that tender friendship for each other which the age inspires."

These extracts prove beyond all question that the first contact with the outer world called into activity two of Shelley's strongest moral qualities—his hatred of tyranny and brutal force in any form, and his profound sentiment of friendship. The admiring love of women, which marked him no less strongly, and which made him second only to Shakespere in the sympathetic delineation of a noble feminine ideal, had been already developed by his deep affection for his mother and sisters. It is said that he could not receive a letter from them without manifest joy.

"Shelley," says Medwin, "was at this time tall for his

age, slightly and delicately built, and rather narrow-chested, with a complexion fair and ruddy, a face rather long than oval. His features, not regularly handsome, were set off by a profusion of silky brown hair, that curled naturally. The expression of his countenance was one of exceeding sweetness and innocence. His blue eyes were very large and prominent. They were at times, when he was abstracted, as he often was in contemplation, dull, and as it were, insensible to external objects ; at others they flashed with the fire of intelligence. His voice was soft and low, but broken in its tones,—when anything much interested him, harsh and immodulated ; and this peculiarity he never lost. He was naturally calm, but when he heard of or read of some flagrant act of injustice, oppression, or cruelty, then indeed the sharpest marks of horror and indignation were visible in his countenance."

Such as the child was, we shall find the man to have remained unaltered through the short space of life allowed him. Loving, innocent, sensitive, secluded from the vulgar concerns of his companions, strongly moralized after a peculiar and inborn type of excellence, drawing his inspirations from Nature and from his own soul in solitude, Shelley passed across the stage of this world, attended by a splendid vision which sustained him at a perilous height above the kindly race of men. The penalty of this isolation he suffered in many painful episodes. The reward he reaped in a measure of more authentic prophecy, and in a nobler realization of his best self, than could be claimed by any of his immediate contemporaries.

CHAPTER II.

ETON AND OXFORD.

In 1805 Shelley went from Sion House to Eton. At this time Dr. Keate was headmaster, and Shelley's tutor was a Mr. Bethel, "one of the dullest men in the establishment." At Eton Shelley was not popular either with his teachers or his elder school-fellows, although the boys of his own age are said to have adored him. "He was all passion," writes Mrs. Shelley, "passionate in his resistance to an injury, passionate in his love :" and this vehemence of temperament he displayed by organizing a rebellion against fagging, which no doubt won for him the applause of his juniors and equals. It was not to be expected that a lad intolerant of rule and disregardful of restriction, who neglected punctuality in the performance of his exercises, while he spent his leisure in translating half of Pliny's history, should win the approbation of pedagogues. At the same time the inspired opponent of the fagging system, the scorner of games and muscular amusements, could not hope to find much favour with such martinets of juvenile convention as a public school is wont to breed. At Eton, as elsewhere, Shelley's uncompromising spirit brought him into inconvenient contact with a world of vulgar usage, while his lively fancy invested the commonplaces of reality with dark hues borrowed from his own imagination. Mrs. Shelley says of him, "Tamed by affection, but unconquered by blows, what chance was there that Shelley should be happy at a public school?" This sentence probably contains the pith of what he afterwards remembered of his own school life, and there is no doubt that a nature like his, at once loving and high-spirited, had much to suffer. It was a mistake, however, to suppose that at Eton there were any serious blows to bear, or to assume that laws of love which might have led a spirit so gentle as Shelley's, were adapted to the common stuff of which the English boy is formed. The latter mistake Shelley made continually throughout his youth; and only the advance of years tempered his passionate enthusiasm into a sober zeal for the improvement of mankind by rational methods. We may also trace at this early epoch of his life that untamed intellectual ambition—that neglect of the immediate and detailed for the transcendental and universal—which was a marked characteristic of his genius, leading him to fly at the highest while he overleaped the facts of ordinary human life. "From his earliest years," says Mrs. Shelley, "all his amusements and occupations were of a daring, and in one sense of the term, lawless nature. He delighted to exert his powers, not as a boy, but as a man; and so with manly powers and childish wit, he dared and achieved attempts that none of his comrades could even have conceived. His understanding and the early development of imagination never permitted him to mingle in childish plays; and his natural aversion to tyranny prevented him from paying due attention to his school duties. But he was always actively employed; and although his endeavours were prosecuted with puerile precipitancy, yet his aim and thoughts were constantly

directed to those great objects which have employed the
thoughts of the greatest among men ; and though his
studies were not followed up according to school discipline, they were not the less diligently applied to."
This high-soaring ambition was the source both of his
weakness and his strength in art, as well as in his commerce with the world of men. The boy who despised
discipline and sought to extort her secrets from nature by
magic, was destined to become the philanthropist who
dreamed of revolutionizing society by eloquence, and the
poet who invented in *Prometheus Unbound* forms of
grandeur too colossal to be animated with dramatic life.

A strong interest in experimental science had been
already excited in him at Sion House by the exhibition
of an orrery ; and this interest grew into a passion at
Eton. Experiments in chemistry and electricity, of the
simpler and more striking kind, gave him intense pleasure
—the more so perhaps because they were forbidden. On
one occasion he set the trunk of an old tree on fire
with a burning glass : on another, while he was amusing
himself with a blue flame, his tutor came into the room
and received a severe shock from a highly-charged Leyden
jar. During the holidays Shelley carried on the same
pursuits at Field Place. "His own hands and clothes,"
says Miss Shelley, " were constantly stained and corroded
with acids, and it only seemed too probable that some
day the house would be burned down, or some serious
mischief happen to himself or others from the explosion
of combustibles." This taste for science Shelley long
retained. If we may trust Mr. Hogg's memory, the first
conversation which that friend had with him at Oxford,
consisted almost wholly of an impassioned monologue
from Shelley on the revolution to be wrought by science

in all realms of thought. His imagination was fascinated by the boundless vistas opened to the student of
chemistry. When he first discovered that the four elements were not final, it gave him the acutest pleasure :
and this is highly characteristic of the genius which was
always seeking to transcend and reach the life of life
withdrawn from ordinary gaze. On the other hand he
seems to have delighted in the toys of science, playing
with a solar microscope, and mixing strangest compounds
in his crucibles, without taking the trouble to study any
of its branches systematically. In his later years he
abandoned these pursuits. But a charming reminiscence
of them occurs in that most delightful of his familiar
poems, the *Letter to Maria Gisborne.*

While translating Pliny and dabbling in chemistry,
Shelley was not wholly neglectful of Etonian studies.
He acquired a fluent, if not a correct, knowledge of both
Greek and Latin, and astonished his contemporaries by
the facility with which he produced verses in the latter
language. His powers of memory were extraordinary,
and the rapidity with which he read a book, taking in
seven or eight lines at a glance, and seizing the sense
upon the hint of leading words, was no less astonishing.
Impatient speed and indifference to minutiæ were indeed
among the cardinal qualities of his intellect. To them
we may trace not only the swiftness of his imaginative
flight, but also his frequent satisfaction with the somewhat less than perfect in artistic execution.

That Shelley was not wholly friendless or unhappy at
Eton may be gathered from numerous small circumstances.
Hogg says that his Oxford rooms were full of handsome
leaving books, and that he was frequently visited by old
Etonian acquaintances. We are also told that he spent

the 40*l.* gained by his first novel, *Zastrozzi*, on a farewell
supper to eight school-boy friends.   A few lines, too,
might be quoted from his own poem, the *Boat on the
Serchio*, to prove that he did not entertain a merely dis-
agreeable memory of his school life.[1] Yet the general
experience of Eton must have been painful ; and it is sad
to read of this gentle and pure spirit being goaded by his
coarser comrades into fury, or coaxed to curse his father
and the king for their amusement. It may be worth
mentioning that he was called "the Atheist" at Eton ;
and though Hogg explains this by saying that "the
Atheist" was an official character among the boys, selected
from time to time for his defiance of authority, yet it is
not improbable that Shelley's avowed opinions may even
then have won for him a title which he proudly claimed
in after-life.   To allude to his boyish incantations and
nocturnal commerce with fiends and phantoms would
scarcely be needful, were it not that they seem to have
deeply tinged his imagination.   While describing the
growth of his own genius in the *Hymn to Intellectual
Beauty*, he makes the following reference to circumstances
which might otherwise be trivial :—

> While yet a boy, I sought for ghosts, and sped
>   Thro' many a listening chamber, cave, and ruin,
>   And starlight wood, with fearful steps pursuing
> Hopes of high talk with the departed dead.
> I call'd on poisonous names with which our youth is fed,
>   I was not heard, I saw them not—
>   When, musing deeply on the lot
> Of life, at that sweet time when winds are wooing
>   All vital things that wake to bring
>   News of birds and blossoming,—
>   Sudden, thy shadow fell on me ;
> I shrieked, and clasped my hands in ecstasy !

---

[1] Forman's edition, vol. iv. p. 115.

Among the Eton tutors was one whose name will always
be revered by Shelley's worshippers; for he alone discerned
the rare gifts of the strange and solitary boy, and Shelley
loved him. Dr. Lind was an old man, a physician, and a
student of chemistry. Shelley spent long hours at his
house, conversing with him, and receiving such instruc-
tion in philosophy and science as the grey-haired scholar
could impart. The affection which united them must
have been of no common strength or quality; for when
Shelley lay ill of a fever at Field Place, and had conceived
the probably ill-founded notion that his father intended
to place him in a mad-house, he managed to convey a
message to his friend at Eton, on the receipt of which Dr.
Lind travelled to Horsham, and by his sympathy and skill
restored the sick boy's confidence. It may incidentally
be pointed out that this story, credited as true by Lady
Shelley in her Memorials, shows how early an estrange-
ment had begun between the poet and his father. We
look, moreover, vainly for that mother's influence which
might have been so beneficial to the boy in whom "love
and life were twins, born at one birth." From Dr.
Lind Shelley not only received encouragement to pursue
his chemical studies; but he also acquired the habit
of corresponding with persons unknown to him, whose
opinions he might be anxious to discover or dispute.
This habit, as we shall see in the sequel, determined
Shelley's fate on two important occasions of his life. In
return for the help extended to him at Eton, Shelley con-
ferred undying fame on Dr. Lind; the characters of
Zonaras in *Prince Athanase*, and of the hermit in *Laon
and Cythna*, are portraits painted by the poet of his boyhood's friend.

The months which elapsed between Eton and Oxford

c

were an important period in Shelley's life. At this time
a boyish liking for his cousin, Harriet Grove, ripened into
real attachment; and though there was perhaps no formal
engagement between them, the parents on both sides
looked with approval on their love. What it concerns us
to know about this early passion, is given in a letter from
a brother of Miss Grove. " Bysshe was at that time (just
after leaving Eton) more attached to my sister Harriet
than I can express, and I recollect well the moonlight
walks we four had at Strode and also at St. Irving's; that,
I think was the name of the place, then the Duke of
Norfolk's, at Horsham." For some time after the date
mentioned in this letter, Shelley and Miss Grove kept up
an active correspondence; but the views he expressed on
speculative subjects soon began to alarm her. She consulted her mother and her father, and the engagement was
broken off. The final separation does not seem to have
taken place until the date of Shelley's expulsion from
Oxford; and not the least cruel of the pangs he had to
suffer at that period, was the loss of one to whom he had
given his whole heart unreservedly. The memory of
Miss Grove long continued to haunt his imagination, nor
is there much doubt that his first unhappy marriage was
contracted while the wound remained unhealed. The
name of Harriet Westbrook and something in her face
reminded him of Harriet Grove; it is even still uncertain
to which Harriet the dedication of Queen Mab is
addressed.[1]

In his childhood Shelley scribbled verses with fluency
by no means unusual in the case of forward boys; and we
have seen that at Sion House he greedily devoured the
sentimental novels of the day. His favourite poets at the

[1] See Medwin, vol. i. p. 68.

time of which I am now writing, were Monk Lewis and
Southey; his favourite books in prose were romances by
Mrs. Radcliffe and Godwin. He now began to yearn for
fame and publicity. Miss Shelley speaks of a play written
by her brother and her sister Elizabeth, which was sent to
Matthews the comedian, and courteously returned as unfit
for acting. She also mentions a little volume of her own
verses, which the boy had printed with the tell-tale name
of "H—ll—n Sh—ll—y" on the title-page. Medwin
gives a long account of a poem on the story of the
Wandering Jew, composed by him in concert with
Shelley during the winter of 1809—1810. They sent the
manuscript to Thomas Campbell, who returned it with the
observation that it contained but two good lines :—

> It seemed as if an angel's sigh
> Had breathed the plaintive symphony.

Undeterred by this adverse criticism Shelley subsequently
offered *The Wandering Jew* to two publishers, Messrs.
Ballantyne and Co. of Edinburgh, and Mr. Stockdale of
Pall Mall; but it remained in MS. at Edinburgh till
1831, when a portion was printed in *Fraser's Magazine.*
Just before leaving Eton he finished his novel of
Zastrozzi, which some critics trace to its source in *Zofloya
the Moor,* perused by him at Sion House. The most
astonishing fact about this incoherent medley of mad sentiment is that it served to furnish forth the 40*l.* Eton
supper already spoken of, that it was duly ushered into
the world of letters by Messrs. Wilkie and Robinson on
the 5th of June, 1810, and that it was seriously reviewed.
The dates of Shelley's publications now come fast and frequent. In the late summer of 1810 he introduced himself to Mr. J. J. Stockdale, the then fashionable publisher

of poems and romances, at his house of business in Pall
Mall. With characteristic impetuosity the young author
implored assistance in a difficulty. He had commissioned
a printer in Horsham to strike off the astounding number
of 1480 copies of a volume of poems; and he had no
money to pay the printer's bill. Would Stockdale help
him out of this dilemma, by taking up the quires and duly
ushering the book into the world? Throughout his life
Shelley exercised a wonderful fascination over the people
with whom he came in contact, and almost always won
his way with them as much by personal charm as by
determined and impassioned will. Accordingly on this
occasion Stockdale proved accommodating. The Horsham
printer was somehow satisfied; and on the 17th of September, 1810, the little book came out with the title of *Original
Poetry, by Victor and Cazire.* This volume has disappeared;
and much fruitless conjecture has been expended upon the
question of Shelley's collaborator in his juvenile attempt.
Cazire stands for some one; probably it is meant to represent a woman's name, and that woman may have been
either Elizabeth Shelley or Harriet Grove. The *Original
Poetry* had only been launched a week, when Stockdale
discovered on a closer inspection of the book that it contained some verses well known to the world as the production of M. G. Lewis. He immediately communicated
with Shelley, and the whole edition was suppressed—not,
however, before about one hundred copies had passed into
circulation. To which of the collaborators this daring act
of petty larceny was due, we know not; but we may be
sure that Shelley satisfied Stockdale on the point of piracy,
since the publisher saw no reason to break with him.
On the 14th of November in the same year he issued
Shelley's second novel from his press, and entered into

negotiations with him for the publication of more poetry. The new romance was named *St. Irvyne, or the Rosicrucian*. This tale, no less unreadable than *Zastrozzi*, and even more chaotic in its plan, contained a good deal of poetry, which has been incorporated in the most recent editions of Shelley's works. A certain interest attaches to it as the first known link between Shelley and William Godwin, for it was composed under the influence of the latter's novel, *St. Leon*. The title, moreover, carries us back to those moonlight walks with Harriet Grove alluded to above. Shelley's earliest attempts in literature have but little value for the student of poetry, except in so far as they illustrate the psychology of genius and its wayward growth. Their intrinsic merit is almost less than nothing, and no one could predict from their perusal the course which the future poet of *The Cenci* and *Epipsychidion* was to take. It might indeed be argued that the defects of his great qualities, the over-ideality, the haste, the incoherence, and the want of grasp on narrative, are glaringly apparent in these early works. But while this is true, the qualities themselves are absent. A cautious critic will only find food in *Zastrozzi* and *St. Irvyne* for wondering how such flowers and fruits of genius could have lain concealed within a germ apparently so barren. There is even less of the real Shelley discernible in these productions, than of the real Byron in the *Hours of Idleness*.

In the Michaelmas Term of 1810 Shelley was matriculated as a Commoner of University College, Oxford ; and very soon after his arrival he made the acquaintance of a man who was destined to play a prominent part in his subsequent history, and to bequeath to posterity the most brilliant, if not in all respects the most trustworthy, record of his marvellous youth. Thomas Jefferson Hogg was unlike Shelley in temperament and tastes. His feet were always planted on the earth, while Shelley flew aloft to heaven with singing robes around him, or the mantle of the prophet on his shoulders.[1] Hogg had much of the cynic in his nature ; he was a shrewd man of the world, and a caustic humorist. Positive and practical, he chose the beaten path of life, rose to eminence as a lawyer, and cherished the Church and State opinions of a staunch Tory. Yet, though he differed so essentially from the divine poet, he understood the greatness of Shelley at a glance, and preserved for us a record of his friend's early days, which is incomparable for the vividness of its portraiture. The pages which narrate Shelley's course of life at Oxford have all the charm of a romance. No novel indeed is half so delightful as that picture, at once affectionate and satirical, tender and humorous, extravagant and delicately shaded, of the student life enjoyed together for a few short months by the inseparable friends. To make extracts from a masterpiece of such consummate workmanship is almost painful. Future biographers of Shelley, writing on a scale adequate to the greatness of their subject, will be content to lay their pens down for a season at this point, and let Hogg tell the tale in his own wayward but inimitable fashion. I must confine myself to a few quotations and a barren abstract, referring my readers to the ever-memorable pages 48—286 of Hogg's first volume, for the life that cannot be transferred to these.

" At the commencement of Michaelmas term," says this

---

[1] He told Trelawny that he had been attracted to Shelley simply by his " rare talents as a scholar ; " and Trelawny has recorded his opinion that Hogg's portrait of their friend was faithful, in spite of a total want of sympathy with his poetic genius. This testimony is extremely valuable.

biographer, "that is, at the end of October, in the year 1810, I happened one day to sit next to a freshman at dinner; it was his first appearance in hall. His figure was slight, and his aspect remarkably youthful, even at our table, where all were very young. He seemed thoughtful and absent. He ate little, and had no acquaintance with any one." The two young men began a conversation, which turned upon the respective merits of German and Italian poetry, a subject they neither of them knew anything about. After dinner it was continued in Hogg's rooms, where Shelley soon led the talk to his favourite topic of science. " As I felt, in truth, but a slight interest in the subject of his conversation, I had leisure to examine, and I may add, to admire, the appearance of my very extraordinary guest. It was a sum of many contradictions. His figure was slight and fragile, and yet his bones and joints were large and strong. He was tall, but he stooped so much, that he seemed of a low stature. His clothes were expensive, and made according to the most approved mode of the day ; but they were tumbled, rumpled, unbrushed. His gestures were abrupt, and sometimes violent, occasionally even awkward, yet more frequently gentle and graceful. His complexion was delicate, and almost feminine, of the purest red and white ; yet he was tanned and freckled by exposure to the sun, having passed the autumn, as he said, in shooting. His features, his whole face, and particularly his head, were, in fact, unusually small ; yet the last *appeared* of a remarkable bulk, for his hair was long and bushy, and in fits of absence, and in the agonies (if I may use the word) of anxious thought, he often rubbed it fiercely with his hands, or passed his fingers quickly through his locks unconsciously, so that it was singularly wild and rough. In times when it was the mode to imi-

tate stage-coachmen as closely as possible in costume, and
when the hair was invariably cropped, like that of our
soldiers, this eccentricity was very striking. His features
were not symmetrical (the mouth, perhaps, excepted), yet
was the effect of the whole extremely powerful. They
breathed an animation, a fire, an enthusiasm, a vivid and
preternatural intelligence, that I never met with in any
other countenance. Nor was the moral expression less
beautiful than the intellectual ; for there was a softness, a
delicacy, a gentleness, and especially (though this will
surprise many) that air of profound religious veneration,
that characterizes the best works, and chiefly the frescoes
(and into these they infused their whole souls), of the great
masters of Florence and of Rome. I recognized the very
peculiar expression in these wonderful productions long
afterwards, and with a satisfaction mingled with much
sorrow, for it was after the decease of him in whose countenance I had first observed it."

In another place Hogg gives some details which complete the impression of Shelley's personal appearance, and
which are fully corroborated by Trelawny's recollections of
a later date. " There were many striking contrasts in the
character and behaviour of Shelley, and one of the most
remarkable was a mixture, or alternation, of awkwardness
with agility—of the clumsy with the graceful. He would
stumble in stepping across the floor of a drawing-room ;
he would trip himself up on a smooth-shaven grass-plot,
and he would tumble in the most inconceivable manner
in ascending the commodious, facile, and well-carpeted
staircase of an elegant mansion, so as to bruise his nose or
his lip on the upper steps, or to tread upon his hands, and
even occasionally to disturb the composure of a well-bred
footman ; on the contrary, he would often glide without

collision through a crowded assembly, thread with unerring dexterity a most intricate path, or securely and rapidly tread the most arduous and uncertain ways."

This word-portrait corresponds in its main details to the descriptions furnished by other biographers, who had the privilege of Shelley's friendship. His eyes were blue, unfathomably dark and lustrous. His hair was brown; but very early in life it became grey, while his unwrinkled face retained to the last a look of wonderful youth. It is admitted on all sides that no adequate picture was ever painted of him. Mulready is reported to have said that he was too beautiful to paint. And yet, although so singularly lovely, he owed less of his charm to regularity of feature or to grace of movement, than to an indescribable personal fascination. One further detail Hogg pointedly insists upon. Shelley's voice " was excruciating; it was intolerably shrill, harsh, and discordant." This is strongly stated; but, though the terms are certainly exaggerated, I believe that we must trust this first impression made on Shelley's friend. There is a considerable mass of convergent testimony to the fact that Shelley's voice was high pitched, and that when he became excited, he raised it to a scream. The epithets "shrill," "piercing," "penetrating," frequently recur in the descriptions given of it. At the same time its quality seems to have been less dissonant than thrilling; there is abundance of evidence to prove that he could modulate it exquisitely in the reading of poetry, and its tone proved no obstacle to the persuasive charms of his eloquence in conversation. Like all finely tempered natures, he vibrated in harmony with the subjects of his thought. Excitement made his utterance shrill and sharp. Deep feeling or the sense of beauty lowered its tone to richness; but the *timbre* was always acute, in sympathy

with his intense temperament. All was of one piece in
Shelley's nature. This peculiar voice, varying from
moment to moment and affecting different sensibilities in
divers ways, corresponds to the high-strung passion of his
life, his fine-drawn and ethereal fancies, and the clear
vibrations of his palpitating verse. Such a voice, far-
reaching, penetrating, and unearthly, befitted one who
lived in rarest ether on the topmost heights of human
thought.

The acquaintance begun that October evening soon
ripened into close friendship. Shelley and Hogg from
this time forward spent a large part of their days and
nights together in common studies, walks, and conversa-
tions. It was their habit to pass the morning, each in his
own rooms, absorbed in private reading. At one o'clock
they met and lunched, and then started for long rambles
in the country. Shelley frequently carried pistols with
him upon these occasions, and would stop to fix his father's
franks upon convenient trees and shoot at them. The
practice of pistol-shooting, adopted so early in his life, was
afterwards one of his favourite amusements in the company
of Byron. Hogg says that in his use of fire-arms he was
extraordinarily careless. " How often have I lamented that
Nature, which so rarely bestows upon the world a creature
endowed with such marvellous talents, ungraciously rendered the gift less precious by implanting a fatal taste for
perilous recreations, and a thoughtlessness in the pursuit
of them, that often caused his existence from one day to
another to seem in itself miraculous." On their return from
these excursions the two friends, neither of whom cared
for dining in the College Hall, drank tea and supped
together, Shelley's rooms being generally chosen as the
scene of their symposia.

These rooms are described as a perfect palace of confusion—chaos on chaos heaped of chemical apparatus, books, electrical machines, unfinished manuscripts, and furniture worn into holes by acids. It was perilous to use the poet's drinking-vessels, lest perchance a seven-shilling piece half dissolved in *aqua regia* should lurk at the bottom of the bowl. Handsome razors were used to cut the lids of wooden boxes, and valuable books served to support lamps or crucibles; for in his vehement precipitation Shelley always laid violent hands on what he found convenient to the purpose of the moment. Here the friends talked and read until late in the night. Their chief studies at this time were in Locke and Hume and the French essayists. Shelley's bias toward metaphysical speculation was beginning to assert itself. He read the School Logic with avidity, and practised himself without intermission in dialectical discussion. Hogg observes, what is confirmed by other testimony, that in reasoning Shelley never lost sight of the essential bearings of the topic in dispute, never condescended to personal or captious arguments, and was Socratically bent on following the dialogue wherever it might lead, without regard for consequences. Plato was another of their favourite authors; but Hogg expressly tells us that they only approached the divine philosopher through the medium of translations. It was not until a later period that Shelley studied his dialogues in the original: but the substance of them, seen through Mdme. Dacier's version, acted powerfully on the poet's sympathetic intellect. In fact, although at this time he had adopted the conclusions of materialism, he was at heart all through his life an idealist. Therefore the mixture of the poet and the sage in Plato fascinated him. The doctrine of *anam-*

nesis, which offers so strange a vista to speculative reverie,
by its suggestion of an earlier existence in which our knowledge was acquired, took a strong hold upon his imagination;
he would stop in the streets to gaze wistfully at babies,
wondering whether their newly imprisoned souls were not
replete with the wisdom stored up in a previous life.

In the acquisition of knowledge he was then as ever un-
relaxing. " No student ever read more assiduously. He
was to be found, book in hand, at all hours ; reading in
season and out of season ; at table, in bed, and especially
during a walk ; not only in the quiet country, and in retired
paths ; not only at Oxford, in the public walks, and High
Street, but in the most crowded thoroughfares of London.
Nor was he less absorbed by the volume that was open
before him, in Cheapside, in Cranbourne Alley, or in
Bond Street, than in a lonely lane, or a secluded library.
Sometimes a vulgar fellow would attempt to insult or annoy
the eccentric student in passing. Shelley always avoided
the malignant interruption by stepping aside with his vast
and quiet agility." And again :—" I never beheld eyes
that devoured the pages more voraciously than his ; I am
convinced that two-thirds of the period of day and night
were often employed in reading. It is no exaggeration to
affirm, that out of the twenty-four hours, he frequently
read sixteen. At Oxford, his diligence in this respect was
exemplary, but it greatly increased afterwards, and I
sometimes thought that he carried it to a pernicious excess :
I am sure, at least, that I was unable to keep pace with
him." With Shelley study was a passion, and the acquisition of knowledge was the entrance into a thrice-hallowed
sanctuary. " The irreverent many cannot comprehend the
awe—the careless apathetic worldling cannot imagine the
enthusiasm—nor can the tongue that attempts only to

speak of things visible to the bodily eye, express the mighty emotion that inwardly agitated him, when he approached, for the first time, a volume which he believed to be replete with the recondite and mystic philosophy of antiquity : his cheeks glowed, his eyes became bright, his whole frame trembled, and his entire attention was immediately swallowed up in the depths of contemplation. The rapid and vigorous conversion of his soul to intellect can only be compared with the instantaneous ignition and combustion, which dazzle the sight, when a bundle of dry reeds, or other light inflammable substance, is thrown upon a fire already rich with accumulated heat."

As at Eton, so at Oxford, Shelley refused to keep the beaten track of prescribed studies, or to run in ordinary grooves of thought. The mere fact that Aristotle was a duty, seems to have disgusted him with the author of the Organon, from whom, had his works been prohibited to undergraduates, he would probably have been eager to learn much. For mathematics and jurisprudence he evinced a marked distaste. The common business of the English Parliament had no attraction for him, and he read few newspapers. While his mind was keenly interested in great political questions, he could not endure the trivial treatment of them in the daily press, and cared far more for principles than for the incidents of party warfare. Here again he showed that impatience of detail, and that audacity of self-reliant genius, which were the source of both his weakness and his strength. He used to speak with aversion of a Parliamentary career, and told Hogg that though this had been suggested to him, as befitting his position, by the Duke of Norfolk, he could never bring himself to mix with the rabble of the House. It is none the less true, however, that he entertained some vague notion of eventually succeeding to his father's seat.

Combined with his eager intellectual activity, there was something intermittent and fitful in the working of his mental faculties. Hogg, in particular, mentions one of his habits in a famous passage, which, since it brings the two friends vividly before us, may here be quoted. " I was enabled to continue my studies afterwards in the evening, in consequence of a very remarkable peculiarity. My young and energetic friend was then overcome by extreme drowsiness, which speedily and completely vanquished him ; he would sleep from two to four hours, often so soundly that his slumbers resembled a deep lethargy ; he lay occasionally upon the sofa, but more commonly stretched upon the rug before a large fire, like a cat ; and his little round head was exposed to such a fierce heat, that I used to wonder how he was able to bear it. Sometimes I have interposed some shelter, but rarely with any permanent effect ; for the sleeper usually contrived to turn himself, and to roll again into the spot where the fire glowed the brightest. His torpor was generally profound, but he would sometimes discourse incoherently for a long while in his sleep. At six he would suddenly compose himself, even in the midst of a most animated narrative, or of earnest discussion ; and he would lie buried in entire forgetfulness, in a sweet and mighty oblivion, until ten, when he would suddenly start up, and, rubbing his eyes with great violence, and passing his fingers swiftly through his long hair, would enter at once into a vehement argument, or begin to recite verses, either of his own composition or from the works of others, with a rapidity and an energy that were often quite painful."

Shelley's moral qualities are described with no less enthusiasm than his intellectual and physical beauty by the friend from whom I have already drawn so largely. Love was the root and basis of his nature : this love, first developed as domestic affection, next as friendship, then as a youth's passion, now began to shine with steady lustre as an all-embracing devotion to his fellow-men. There is something inevitably chilling in the words "benevolence" and "philanthropy." A disillusioned world is inclined to look with languid approbation on the former, and to disbelieve in the latter. Therefore I will not use them to describe that intense and glowing passion of unselfishness, which throughout his life led Shelley to find his strongest interests in the joys and sorrows of his fellow-creatures, which inflamed his imagination with visions of humanity made perfect, and which filled his days with sweet deeds of unnumbered charities. I will rather collect from the pages of his friend's biography a few passages recording the first impression of his character, the memory of which may be carried by the reader through the following brief record of his singular career :—

" His speculations were as wild as the experience of twenty-one years has shown them to be ; but the zealous earnestness for the augmentation of knowledge, and the glowing philanthropy and boundless benevolence that marked them, and beamed forth in the whole deportment of that extraordinary boy, are not less astonishing than they would have been if the whole of his glorious antici- pations had been prophetic ; for these high qualities, at least, I have never found a parallel."

" In no individual perhaps was the moral sense ever more completely developed than in Shelley ; in no being was the perception of right and of wrong more acute."

" As his love of intellectual pursuits was vehement, and the vigour of his genius almost celestial, so were the purity and sanctity of his life most conspicuous."

" I never knew any one so prone to admire as he was, in whom the principle of veneration was so strong."

" I have had the happiness to associate with some of the best specimens of gentlemen; but with all due deference for those admirable persons (may my candour and my preference be pardoned), I can affirm that Shelley was almost the only example I have yet found that was never wanting, even in the most minute particular, of the infinite and various observances of pure, entire, and perfect gentility."

" Shelley was actually offended, and indeed more indignant than would appear to be consistent with the singular mildness of his nature, at a coarse and awkward jest, especially if it were immodest, or uncleanly; in the latter case his anger was unbounded, and his uneasiness pre-eminent; he was, however, sometimes vehemently delighted by exquisite and delicate sallies, particularly with a fanciful, and perhaps somewhat fantastical facetiousness—possibly the more because he was himself utterly incapable of pleasantry."

" I never could discern in him any more than two fixed principles. The first was a strong irrepressible love of liberty; of liberty in the abstract, and somewhat after the pattern of the ancient republics, without reference to the English constitution, respecting which he knew little and cared nothing, heeding it not at all. The second was an equally ardent love of toleration of all opinions, but more especially of religious opinions; of toleration, complete, entire, universal, unlimited; and, as a deduction and corollary from which latter principle, he felt an intense abhorrence of persecution of every kind, public or private."

The testimony in the foregoing extracts as to Shelley's purity and elevation of moral character is all the stronger, because it is given by a man not over-inclined to praise, and of a temperament as unlike the poet's as possible. If we were to look only upon this side of his portrait, we should indeed be almost forced to use the language of his most enthusiastic worshippers, and call him an archangel. But it must be admitted that, though so pure and gentle and exalted, Shelley's virtues were marred by his eccentricity, by something at times approaching madness, which paralysed his efficiency by placing him in a glaringly false relation to some of the best men of the world around him. He possessed certain good qualities in excess; for, though it sounds paradoxical, it is none the less true that a man may be too tolerant, too fond of liberty : and it was precisely the extravagance of these virtues in Shelley which drove him into acts and utterances so antagonistic to society as to be intolerable.

Of Shelley's poetical studies we hear but little at this epoch. His genius by a stretch of fancy might be compared to one of those double stars which dart blue and red rays of light : for it was governed by two luminaries, poetry and metaphysics ; and at this time the latter seems to have been in the ascendant. It is, however, interesting to learn that he read and re-read Landor's *Gebir*— stronger meat than either Southey's epics or the ghost-lyrics of Monk Lewis. Hogg found him one day busily engaged in correcting proofs of some original poems. Shelley asked his friend what he thought of them, and Hogg answered that it might be possible by a little alteration to turn them into capital burlesques. This idea took the young poet's fancy; and the friends between them soon effected a metamorphosis in Shelley's serious verses, by which they became unmistakably ridiculous. Having achieved their purpose, they now bethought them of the proper means of publication. Upon whom should the poems, a medley of tyrannicide and revolutionary raving, be fathered? Peg Nicholson, a mad washerwoman, had recently attempted George the Third's life with a carving-knife. No more fitting author could be found. They would give their pamphlet to the world as her work, edited by an admiring nephew. The printer appreciated the joke no less than the authors of it. He provided splendid paper and magnificent type; and before long the book of nonsense was in the hands of Oxford readers. It sold for the high price of half-a-crown a copy; and, what is hardly credible, the gownsmen received it as a genuine production. " It was indeed a kind of fashion to be seen reading it in public, as a mark of nice discernment, of a delicate and fastidious taste in poetry, and the best criterion of a choice spirit." Such was the genesis of *Posthumous Fragments of Margaret Nicholson*, edited by John Fitz Victor. The name of the supposititious nephew reminds us of *Original Poems* by Victor and Cazire, and raises the question whether the poems in that lost volume may not have partly furnished forth this Oxford travesty.

Shelley's next publication, or quasi-publication, was neither so innocent in substance nor so pleasant in its consequences. After leaving Eton, he continued the habit, learned from Dr. Lind, of corresponding with distinguished persons whom he did not personally know. Thus we find him about this time addressing Miss Felicia Browne (afterwards Mrs. Hemans) and Leigh Hunt. He plied his correspondents with all kinds of questions; and as the dialectical interest was uppermost at Oxford, he now endeavoured to engage them in discussions on philosophical and religious topics. We have seen that his favourite authors were Locke, Hume, and the French materialists. With the impulsiveness peculiar to his nature, he adopted the negative conclusions of a shallow nominalistic philosophy. It was a fundamental point with him to regard all questions, however sifted and settled by the wise of former ages, as still open; and in his inordinate thirst for liberty, he rejoiced to be the Deicide of a pernicious theological delusion. In other words, he passed at Oxford by one leap from a state of indifferentism with regard to Christianity, into an attitude of vehement antagonism. With a view to securing answers to his missives, he printed a short abstract of Hume's and other arguments against the existence of a Deity, presented in a series of propositions, and signed with a mathematically important "Q. E. D." This document he forwarded to his proposed antagonists, expressing his inability to answer its arguments, and politely requesting them to help him. When it so happened that any incautious correspondents acceded to this appeal, Shelley fell with merciless severity upon their feeble and commonplace reasoning. The little pamphlet of two pages was entitled *The Necessity of Atheism;* and its proposed publication, beyond the limits of private circulation already described, is proved by an advertisement (Feb. 9, 1811) in the *Oxford University and City Herald.* It was not, however, actually offered for sale.

A copy of this syllabus reached a Fellow of another college, who made the Master of University acquainted with the fact. On the morning of March 25, 1811,

Shelley was sent for to the Senior Common Room, and asked whether he acknowledged himself to be the author of the obnoxious pamphlet. On his refusal to answer this question, he was served with a formal sentence of expulsion duly drawn up and sealed. The college authorities have been blamed for unfair dealing in this matter. It is urged that they ought to have proceeded by the legal method of calling witnesses ; and that the sentence was not only out of all proportion to the offence, but that it ought not to have been executed till persuasion had been tried. With regard to the former indictment, I do not think that a young man still *in statu pupillari*, who refused to purge himself of what he must have known to be a serious charge, had any reason to expect from his tutors the formalities of an English court of law. There is no doubt that the Fellows were satisfied of his being the real author ; else they could not have ventured on so summary a measure as expulsion. Their question was probably intended to give the culprit an occasion for apology, of which they foresaw he would not avail himself. With regard to the second, it is true that Shelley was amenable to kindness, and that gentle and wise treatment from men whom he respected, might possibly have brought him to retract his syllabus. But it must be remembered that he despised the Oxford dons with all his heart ; and they were probably aware of this. He was a dexterous, impassioned reasoner, whom they little cared to encounter in argument on such a topic. During his short period of residence, moreover, he had not shown himself so tractable as to secure the good wishes of superiors, who prefer conformity to incommensurable genius. It is likely that they were not averse to getting rid of him as a man dangerous to the peace of their society ; and now they

had a good occasion.　Nor was it to be expected that the
champion and apostle of Atheism—and Shelley was certainly both, in spite of Hogg's attempts to tone down the
purpose of his document—should be unmolested in his
propaganda by the aspirants to fat livings and ecclesiastical dignities.　Real blame, however, attaches to these
men : first, for their dulness to discern Shelley's amiable
qualities ; and, secondly, for the prejudgment of the case
implied in the immediate delivery of their sentence.　Both
Hogg and Shelley accused them, besides, of a gross
brutality, which was, to say the least, unseemly on so
serious an occasion.　At the beginning of this century
the learning and the manners of the Oxford dons were at
a low ebb ; and the Fellows of University College acted
harshly but not altogether unjustly, ignorantly but after
their own kind, in this matter of Shelley's expulsion.
Non ragionam di lor, ma guarda e passa.　Hogg, who stood
by his friend manfully at this crisis, and dared the authorities to deal with him as they had dealt with Shelley,
adding that they had just as much real proof to act upon
in his case, and intimating his intention of returning the
same answer as to the authorship of the pamphlet, was
likewise expelled.　The two friends left Oxford together
by the coach on the morning of the 26th of March.

Shelley felt his expulsion acutely.　At Oxford he had
enjoyed the opportunities of private reading which the
University afforded in those days of sleepy studies and
innocuous examinations.　He delighted in the security of
his "oak," and above all things he found pleasure in the
society of his one chosen friend.　He was now obliged to
exchange these good things for the tumult and discomfort
of London.　His father, after clumsily attempting com-
promises, had forbidden his return to Field Place.　The

whole fabric of his former life was broken up. The last
hope of renewing his engagement with his cousin had to
be abandoned. His pecuniary position was precarious,
and in a short time he was destined to lose the one friend
who had so generously shared his fate. Yet the notion of
recovering his position as a student in one of our great
Universities, of softening his father's indignation, or of
ameliorating his present circumstances by the least con-
cession, never seems to have occurred to him. He had
suffered in the cause of truth and liberty, and he willingly
accepted his martyrdom for conscience' sake.

CHAPTER III.

IT is of some importance at this point to trace the growth
and analyse the substance of Shelley's atheistical opinions.
The cardinal characteristic of his nature was an implacable
antagonism to shams and conventions, which passed too
easily into impatient rejection of established forms as
worse than useless. Born in the stronghold of squire-
archical prejudices, nursed amid the trivial platitudes that
then passed in England for philosophy, his keen spirit
flew to the opposite pole of thought with a recoil that
carried him at first to inconsiderate negation. His passionate love of liberty, his loathing for intolerance, his
impatience of control for self and others, and his vivid
logical sincerity, combined to make him the Quixotic
champion of extreme opinions. He was too fearless to be
wise, too precipitate to suspend his judgment, too convinced of the paramount importance of iconoclasm, to
mature his views in silence. With the unbounded
audacity of youth, he hoped to take the fortresses of
"Anarch Custom" by storm at the first assault. His
favourite ideal was the vision of a youth, Laon or Lionel,
whose eloquence had power to break the bonds of despotism,
as the sun thaws ice upon an April morning. It was
enough, he thought, to hurl the glove of defiance boldly at

the tyrant's face—to sow the *Necessity of Atheism* broadcast on the bench of Bishops, and to depict incest in his
poetry, not because he wished to defend it, but because
society must learn to face the most abhorrent problems with
impartiality. Gifted with a touch as unerring as Ithuriel's
spear for the unmasking of hypocrisy, he strove to lay
bare the very substance of the soul beneath the crust of
dogma and the froth of traditional beliefs; nor does it
seem to have occurred to him that, while he stripped the
rags and patches that conceal the nakedness of ordinary
human nature, he might drag away the weft and woof of
nobler thought. In his poet-philosopher's imagination
there bloomed a wealth of truth and love and beauty so
abounding, that behind the mirage be destroyed, he saw
no blank, but a new Eternal City of the Spirit. He
never doubted whether his fellow-creatures were certain
to be equally fortunate.

Shelley had no faculty for compromise, no perception
of the blended truths and falsehoods through which the
mind of man must gradually win its way from the
obscurity of myths into the clearness of positive knowledge, for ever toiling and for ever foiled, and forced to
content itself with the increasing consciousness of limita-
tions. Brimming over with love for men, he was
deficient in sympathy with the conditions under which
they actually think and feel. Could he but dethrone
the Anarch Custom, the millennium, he argued, would
immediately arrive; nor did he stop to think how different
was the fibre of his own soul from that of the unnumbered
multitudes around him. In his adoration of what he
recognized as living, he retained no reverence for the
ossified experience of past ages. The principle of evolution,
which forms a saving link between the obsolete and the

organically vital, had no place in his logic. The spirit of
the French Revolution, uncompromising, shattering, eager
to build in a day the structure which long centuries of
growth must fashion, was still fresh upon him. We who
have survived the enthusiasms of that epoch, who are
exhausted with its passions, and who have suffered from
its reactive impulses, can scarcely comprehend the vivid
faith and young-eyed joy of aspiration which sustained
Shelley in his flight toward the region of impossible ideals.
For he had a vital faith ; and this faith made the ideals
he conceived, seem possible—faith in the duty and
desirability of overthrowing idols ; faith in the gospel of
liberty, fraternity, equality ; faith in the divine beauty of
nature ; faith in a love that rules the universe ; faith in
the perfectibility of man ; faith in the omnipresent soul,
whereof our souls are atoms ; faith in affection as the
ruling and co-ordinating substance of morality.   The man
who lived by this faith was in no vulgar sense of the word
an Atheist.   When he proclaimed himself to be one, he
pronounced his hatred of a gloomy religion, which had
been the instrument of kings and priests for the enslave-
ment of their fellow-creatures.   As he told his friend
Trelawny, he used the word Atheism "to express his
abhorrence of superstition ; he took it up as a knight took
up a gauntlet, in defiance of injustice."   But Shelley
believed too much to be consistently agnostic.   He
believed so firmly and intensely in his own religion—a
kind of passionate positivism, a creed which seemed to
have no God because it was all God—that he felt convinced he only needed to destroy accepted figments, for the
light which blazed around him to break through and flood
the world with beauty.   Shelley can only be called an
Atheist, in so far as he maintained the inadequacy of

hitherto received conceptions of the Deity, and indignantly
rejected that Moloch of cruelty who is worshipped in
the debased forms of Christianity. He was an Agnostic
only in so far as he proclaimed the impossibility of solving
the insoluble, and knowing the unknowable. His clear
and fearless utterances upon these points place him in the
rank of intellectual heroes. But his own soul, compact of
human faith and love, was far too religious and too
sanguine to merit either epithet as vulgarly applied.

The negative side of Shelley's creed had the moral
value which attaches to all earnest conviction, plain
speech, defiance of convention, and enthusiasm for intellectual liberty at any cost. It was marred, however,
by extravagance, crudity, and presumption. Much that
he would fain have destroyed because he found it
customary, was solid, true, and beneficial. Much that he
thought it desirable to substitute, was visionary, hollow,
and pernicious. He lacked the touchstone of mature
philosophy, whereby to separate the pinchbeck from the
gold of social usage ; and in his intense enthusiasm he
lost his hold on common sense, which might have saved
him from the puerility of arrogant iconoclasm. The
positive side of his creed remains precious, not because it
was logical, or scientific, or coherent, but because it was
an ideal, fervently felt, and penetrated with the whole
life-force of an incomparable nature. Such ideals are
needed for sustaining man upon his path amid the glooms
and shadows of impenetrable ignorance. They form the
seal and pledge of his spiritual dignity, reminding him
that he was not born to live like brutes, or like the brutes
to perish without effort.

> Fatti non foste a viver come bruti,
> Ma per seguir virtude e conoscenza

These criticisms apply to the speculations of Shelley's earlier life, when his crusade against accepted usage was extravagant, and his confidence in the efficacy of mere eloquence to change the world was overweening. The experience of years, however, taught him wisdom without damping his enthusiasm, refined the crudity of his first fervent speculations, and mellowed his philosophy. Had he lived to a ripe age, there is no saying with what clear and beneficent lustre might have shone that light of aspiration which during his turbid youth burned somewhat luridly, and veiled its radiance in the smoke of mere rebelliousness and contradiction.

Hogg and Shelley settled in lodgings at No. 15, Poland Street, soon after their arrival in London. The name attracted Shelley : " it reminded him of Thaddeus of Warsaw and of freedom." He was further fascinated by a gaudy wall-paper of vine-trellises and grapes, which adorned the parlour; and vowed that he would stay there for ever. " For ever," was a word often upon Shelley's lips in the course of his checquered life ; and yet few men have been subject to so many sudden changes through the buffetings of fortune from without and the inconstancy of their own purpose, than he was. His biographer has no little trouble to trace and note with accuracy his perpetual flittings and the names of his innumerable temporary residences. A month had not elapsed before Hogg left him in order to begin his own law studies at York; and Shelley abode " alone in the vine-trellised chamber, where he was to remain, a bright-eyed, restless fox amidst sour grapes, not, as his poetic imagination at first suggested, for ever, but a little while longer."

The records of this first residence in London are

meagre, but not unimportant. We hear of negotiations
and interviews with Mr. Timothy Shelley, all of which
proved unavailing. Shelley would not recede from the
position he had taken up. Nothing would induce him to
break off his intimacy with Hogg, or to place himself
under the tutor selected for him by his father. For
Paley's, or as Mr. Shelley called him "Palley's,"
Evidences he expressed unbounded contempt. The
breach between them gradually widened. Mr. Shelley
at last determined to try the effect of cutting off supplies;
but his son only hardened his heart, and sustained himself by a proud consciousness of martyrdom. I agree
with Shelley's last and best biographer, Mr. W. M.
Rossetti, in his condemnation of the poet's behaviour as a
son. Shelley did not treat his father with the common
consideration due from youth to age; and the only instances of unpardonable bad taste to be found in his
correspondence or the notes of his conversation, are in-
sulting phrases applied to a man who was really more
unfortunate than criminal in his relations to this change-
ling from the realms of faëry. It is not too much to say
that his dislike of his father amounted to derangement;
and certainly some of his suspicions with regard to him
were the hallucinations of a heated fancy. How so just
and gentle a nature was brought into so false a moral
situation, whether by some sudden break-down of confidence in childhood or by a gradually increasing mistrust,
is an interesting but perhaps insoluble problem. We
only know that in his early boyhood Shelley loved his
father so much as to have shown unusual emotion during
his illness on one occasion, but that, while at Eton, he had
already become possessed by a dark suspicion concerning
him. This is proved by the episode of Dr. Lind's visit

during his fever. Then and ever afterwards he expected monstrous treatment at his hands, although the elder gentleman was nothing worse than a muddle-headed squire. It has more than once occurred to me that this fever may have been a turning point in his history, and that a delusion, engendered by delirium, may have fixed itself upon his mind, owing to some imperfection in the process of recovery. But the theory is too speculative and unsupported by proof to be more than passingly alluded to.

At this time Shelley found it difficult to pay his lodgings and buy food. It is said that his sisters saved their pocket-money to support him : and we know that he paid them frequent visits at their school on Clapham Common. It was here that his characteristic hatred of tyranny displayed itself on two occasions. " One day," writes Miss Hellen Shelley, " his ire was greatly excited at a black mark hung round one of our throats, as a penalty for some small misdemeanour. He expressed great disapprobation, more of the system than that one of his sisters should be so punished. Another time he found me, I think, in an iron collar, which certainly was a dreadful instrument of torture in my opinion. It was not worn as a punishment, but because I *poked ;* but Bysshe declared it would make me grow crooked, and ought to be discontinued immediately." The acquaintance which he now made with one of his sister's school friends was destined to lead to most important results.[1] Harriet Westbrook was a girl of sixteen years, remarkably good-looking, with a brilliant pink and white complexion, beautiful brown hair, a pleasant voice, and a cheerful

[1] It is probable that he saw her for the first time in January, 1811.

temper. She was the daughter of a man who kept a coffee-house in Mount Street, nick-named "Jew" West-brook, because of his appearance. She had an elder sister, called Eliza, dark of complexion, and gaunt of figure, with the abundant hair that plays so prominent a part in Hogg's relentless portrait. Eliza, being nearly twice as old as Harriet, stood in the relation of a mother to her. Both of these young ladies, and the "Jew" their father, welcomed Shelley with distinguished kind-ness. Though he was penniless for the nonce, exiled from his home, and under the ban of his family's dis-pleasure, he was still the heir to a large landed fortune and a baronetcy. It was not to be expected that the coffee-house people should look upon him with dis-favour.

Shelley paid Harriet frequent visits both at Mrs. Fen-ning's school and at Mount Street, and soon began a correspondence with her, hoping, as he expressly stated in a letter of a later date, by converting her to his theories, to add his sister and her "to the list of the good, the disinterested, the free." At first she seems to have been horrified at the opinions he expressed; but in this case at least he did not overrate the powers of eloquence. With all the earnestness of an evangelist, he preached his gospel of freethought or atheism, and had the satis-faction of forming his young pupil to his views. He does not seem to have felt any serious inclination for Harriet; but in the absence of other friends, he gladly availed himself of her society. Gradually she became more interesting to him, when he heard mysterious accounts of suffering at home and tyranny at school. This was enough to rouse in Shelley the spirit of Quixotic championship, if not to sow the seeds of love. What

Harriet's ill-treatment really was, no one has been able to discover; yet she used to affirm that her life at this time was so irksome that she contemplated suicide.

During the summer of 1811, Shelley's movements were more than usually erratic, and his mind was in a state of extraordinary restlessness. In the month of May, a kind of accommodation was come to with his father. He received permission to revisit Field Place, and had an allowance made him of 200*l.* a year. His uncle, Captain Pilfold of Cuckfield, was instrumental in effecting this partial reconciliation. Shelley spent some time at his uncle's country house, oscillating between London, Cuckfield, and Field Place, with characteristic rapidity, and paying one flying visit to his cousin Grove at Cwm Elan, near Rhayader, in North Wales. This visit is worth mention, since he now for the first time saw the scenery of waterfalls and mountains. He was, however, too much preoccupied to take much interest in nature. He was divided between his old affection for Miss Grove, his new but somewhat languid interest in Harriet, and a dearly cherished scheme for bringing about a marriage between his sister Elizabeth and his friend Hogg. The letters written to Hogg at this period (vol. i. pp. 387—418), are exceedingly important and interesting, revealing as they do the perturbation of his feelings and the almost morbid excitement of his mind. But they are unluckily so badly edited, whether designedly or by accident, that it would be dangerous to draw minute conclusions from them. As they stand, they raise injurious suspicions, which can only be set at rest by a proper assignment of dates and explanations.

Meanwhile his destiny was shaping itself with a rapidity that plunged him suddenly into decisive and irrevocable action. It is of the greatest moment to ascertain precisely what his feelings were during this summer with regard to Harriet. Hogg has printed two letters in immediate juxtaposition : the first without date, the second with the post-mark of Rhayader. Shelley ends the first epistle thus : " Your jokes on Harriet Westbrook amuse me : it is a common error for people to fancy others in their own situation, but if I know anything about love, I am *not* in love. I have heard from the Westbrooks, both of whom I highly esteem." He begins the second with these words : " You will perhaps see me before you can answer this ; perhaps not ; heaven knows ! I shall certainly come to York, but *Harriet Westbrook* will decide whether now or in three weeks. Her father has persecuted her in a most horrible way, by endeavouring to compel her to go to school. She asked my advice: resistance was the answer, at the same time that I essayed to mollify Mr. W. in vain ! And in consequence of my advice *she* has thrown herself upon *my* protection. I set off for London on Monday. How flattering a distinction !—I am thinking of ten million things at once. What have I said ? I declare, quite *ludicrous.* I advised her to resist. She wrote to say that resistance was useless, but that she would fly with me, and threw herself upon my protection. We shall have 200*l.* a year ; when we find it run short, we must live, I suppose, upon love ! Gratitude and admiration, all demand that I should love her *for ever.* We shall see you at York. I will hear your arguments for matrimonialism, by which I am now almost convinced. I can get lodgings at York, I suppose. Direct to me at Graham's, 18, Sackville Street, Piccadilly." From a letter recently published by Mr. W. M. Rossetti (the University Magazine, Feb.

1878), we further learn that Harriet, having fallen violently in love with her preceptor, had avowed her passion and flung herself into his arms.

It is clear from these documents, first, that Shelley was not deeply in love with Harriet when he eloped with her ; secondly, that he was not prepared for the step ; thirdly, that she induced him to take it ; and fourthly, that he took it under a strong impression of her having been ill-treated. She had appealed to his most powerful passion, the hatred of tyranny. She had excited his admiration by setting conventions at defiance, and showing her readiness to be his mistress. Her confidence called forth his gratitude. Her choice of him for a protector flattered him : and, moreover, she had acted on his advice to carry resistance *à outrance*. There were many good Shelleyan reasons why he should elope with Harriet ; but among them all I do not find that spontaneous and un-sophisticated feeling, which is the substance of enduring love.

In the same series of letters, so incoherently jumbled together by Hogg's carelessness or caprice, Shelley more than once expresses the utmost horror of matrimony. Yet we now find him upon the verge of contracting marriage with a woman whom he did not passionately love, and who had offered herself unreservedly to him. It is worth pausing to observe that even Shelley, fearless and uncompromising as he was in conduct, could not at this crisis practise the principles he so eloquently impressed on others. Yet the point of weakness was honourable. It lay in his respect for women in general, and his tender chivalry for the one woman who had cast herself upon his generosity.[1]

[1] See Shelley's third letter to Godwin (Hogg, ii. p. 63) for another defence of his conduct. " We agreed," &c.

"My unfortunate friend Harriet," he writes under date Aug. 15, 1811, from London, whither he had hurried to arrange the affairs of his elopement, "is yet undecided ; not with respect to me, but to herself. How much, my dear friend, have I to tell you ! In my leisure moments for thought, which since I wrote, have been few, I have considered the important point on which you reprobated my hasty decision. The ties of love and honour are doubtless of sufficient strength to bind congenial souls —they are doubtless indissoluble, but by the brutish force of power ; they are delicate and satisfactory. Yet the arguments of impracticability, and what is even worse, the disproportionate sacrifice which the female is called upon to make—these arguments, which you have urged in a manner immediately irresistible, I cannot withstand. Not that I suppose it to be likely that *I* shall directly be called upon to evince my attachment to either theory. I am become a perfect convert to matrimony, not from temporizing, but from *your* arguments ; nor, much as I wish to emulate your virtues and liken myself to you, do I regret the prejudices of anti-matrimonialism from your example or assertion. No. The *one* argument, which you have urged so often with so much energy ; the sacrifice made by the woman, so disproportioned to any which the man can give—this alone may exculpate me, were it a fault, from uninquiring submission to your superior intellect."

Whether Shelley from his own peculiar point of view was morally justified in twice marrying, is a question of casuistry which has often haunted me. The reasons he alleged in extenuation of his conduct with regard to Harriet, prove the goodness of his heart, his openness to argument, and the delicacy of his unselfishness. But they do not square with his expressed code of conduct ;

nor is it easy to understand how, having found it needful
to submit to custom, for his partner's sake, he should
have gone on denouncing an institution which he
recognized in his own practice. The conclusion seems
to be that, though he despised accepted usage and would
fain have fashioned the world afresh to suit his heart's
desire, the instincts of a loyal gentleman and his practical
good sense were stronger than his theories.

A letter from Shelley's cousin, Mr. C. H. Grove, gives
the details of Harriet's elopement. " When Bysshe finally
came to town to elope with Miss Westbrook, he came as
usual to Lincoln's Inn Fields, and I was his companion on
his visits to her, and finally accompanied them early one
morning—I forget now the month, or the date, but it
might have been September—in a hackney coach to the
Green Dragon, in Gracechurch Street, where we remained
all day, till the hour when the mail-coaches start, when
they departed in the northern mail for York." From
York the young couple made their way at once to Edinburgh, where they were married according to the formalities
of the Scotch law.

Shelley had now committed that greatest of social
crimes in his father's eyes—a *mésalliance*. Supplies and
communications were at once cut off from the prodigal;
and it appears that Harriet and he were mainly dependent
upon the generosity of Captain Pilfold for subsistence.
Even Jew Westbrook, much as he may have rejoiced at
seeing his daughter wedded to the heir of several thousands
a year, buttoned up his pockets, either because he thought
it well to play the part of an injured parent, or because
he was not certain about Shelley's expectations. He afterwards made the Shelleys an allowance of 200*l.* a year, and
early in 1812 Shelley says that he is in receipt of twice that

income. Whence we may conclude that both fathers before
long relented to the extent of the sum above mentioned.

In spite of temporary impecuniosity, the young people
lived happily enough in excellent lodgings in George
Street. Hogg, who joined them early in September,
has drawn a lively picture of their domesticity. Much
of the day was spent in reading aloud; for Harriet, who
had a fine voice and excellent lungs, was never happy
unless she was allowed to read and comment on her
favourite authors. Shelley sometimes fell asleep during
the performance of these rites; but when he woke
refreshed with slumber, he was no less ready than at
Oxford to support philosophical paradoxes with impassioned and persuasive eloquence. He began to teach
Harriet Latin, set her to work upon the translation of a
French story by Madame Cottin, and for his own part
executed a version of one of Buffon's treatises. The
sitting-room was full of books. It was one of Shelley's
peculiarities to buy books wherever he went, regardless of
their volume or their cost. These he was wont to leave
behind, when the moment arrived for a sudden departure
from his temporary abode; so that, as Hogg remarks, a
fine library might have been formed from the waifs and
strays of his collections scattered over the three kingdoms.
This quiet course of life was diversified by short rambles
in the neighbourhood of Edinburgh, and by many episodes
related with Hogg's caustic humour. On the whole, the
impression left upon the reader's mind is that Shelley and
Harriet were very happy together at this period, and that
Harriet was a charming and sweet-tempered girl, somewhat
too much given to the study of trite ethics, and slightly
deficient in sensibility, but otherwise a fit and soothing
companion for the poet.

They were not, however, content to remain in Edinburgh. Hogg was obliged to leave that city, in order to resume his law studies at York, and Shelley's programme of life at this period imperatively required the society of his chosen comrade. It was therefore decided that the three friends should settle at York, to remain "for ever" in each other's company. They started in a post-chaise, the good Harriet reading aloud novels by the now forgotten Holcroft with untiring energy, to charm the tedium of the journey. At York more than one cloud obscured their triune felicity. In the first place they were unfortunate in their choice of lodgings. In the second Shelley found himself obliged to take an expensive journey to London, in the fruitless attempt to come to some terms with his father's lawyer, Mr. Whitton. Mr. Timothy Shelley was anxious to bind his erratic son down to a settlement of the estates, which, on his own death, would pass into the poet's absolute control. He suggested numerous arrangements ; and not long after the date of Shelley's residence in York, he proposed to make him an immediate allowance of 2000*l.*, if Shelley would but consent to entail the land on his heirs male. This offer was indignantly refused. Shelley recognized the truth that property is a trust far more than a possession, and would do nothing to tie up so much command over labour, such incalculable potentialities of social good or evil, for an unborn being of whose opinions he knew nothing. This is only one among many instances of his readiness to sacrifice ease, comfort, nay, the bare necessities of life, for principle.

On his return to York, Shelley found a new inmate established in their lodgings. The incomparable Eliza, who was henceforth doomed to guide his destinies to an obscure catastrophe, had arrived from London. Harriet believed her sister to be a paragon of beauty, good sense, and propriety. She obeyed her elder sister like a mother ; never questioned her wisdom ; and foolishly allowed her to interpose between herself and her husband. Hogg had been told before her first appearance in the friendly circle that Eliza was "beautiful, exquisitely beautiful ; an elegant figure, full of grace ; her face was lovely,—dark, bright eyes ; jet-black hair, glossy ; a crop upon which she bestowed the care it merited,—almost all her time ; and she was so sensible, so amiable, so good !" Now let us listen to the account he has himself transmitted of this woman, whom certainly he did not love, and to whom poor Shelley had afterwards but little reason to feel gratitude. "She was older than I had expected, and she looked much older than she was. The lovely face was seamed with the small-pox, and of a dead white, as faces so much marked and scarred commonly are ; as white indeed as a mass of boiled rice, but of a dingy hue, like rice boiled in dirty water. The eyes were dark, but dull, and without meaning ; the hair was black and glossy, but coarse, and there was the admired crop—a long crop, much like the tail of a horse—a switch tail. The fine figure was meagre, prim, and constrained. The beauty, the grace, and the elegance existed, no doubt, in their utmost perfection, but only in the imagination of her partial young sister. Her father, as Harriet told me, was familiarly called 'Jew Westbrook,' and Eliza greatly resembled one of the dark-eyed daughters of Judah."

This portrait is drawn, no doubt, with an unfriendly hand ; and, in Hogg's biography, each of its sarcastic touches is sustained with merciless reiteration, whenever the mention of Eliza's name is necessary. We hear, moreover, how she taught the blooming Harriet to fancy that she was the victim of her nerves, how she checked her favourite studies, and how she ruled the household by continual reference to a Mrs. Grundy of her earlier experience. " What would Miss Warne say ?" was as often on her lips, if we may credit Hogg, as the brush and comb were in her hands.

The intrusion of Eliza disturbed the harmony of Shelley's circle ; but it is possible that there were deeper reasons for the abrupt departure which he made from York with his wife and her sister in November, 1811. One of his biographers asserts with categorical precision that Shelley had good cause to resent Hogg's undue familiarity with Harriet, and refers to a curious composition, published by Hogg as a continuation of Goethe's *Werther*, but believed by Mr. McCarthy to have been a letter from the poet to his friend, in confirmation of his opinion.[1] However this may be, the precipitation with which the Shelleys quitted York, scarcely giving Hogg notice of their resolution, is insufficiently accounted for in his biography.

The destination of the travellers was Keswick. Here they engaged lodgings for a time, and then moved into a furnished house.   Probably Shelley was attracted to the lake country as much by the celebrated men who lived there, as by the beauty of its scenery, and the cheapness of its accommodation. He had long entertained an admiration for Southey's poetry, and was now beginning to study Wordsworth and Coleridge.   But if he hoped for much companionship with the literary lions of the lakes, he was disappointed.   Coleridge was absent, and missed making his acquaintance—a circumstance he afterwards regretted, saying that he could have been more useful to the young

[1] McCarthy's Shelley's Early Life, p. 117.

poet and metaphysician than Southey. De Quincey,
though he writes ambiguously upon this point, does not
seem to have met Shelley. Wordsworth paid him no
attention; and though he saw a good deal of Southey,
this intimacy changed Shelley's early liking for the man
and poet into absolute contempt. It was not likely that
the cold methodical student, the mechanical versifier, and
the political turncoat, who had outlived all his earlier
illusions, should retain the goodwill of such an Ariel as
Shelley, in whose brain *Queen Mab* was already simmering.
Life at Keswick began to be monotonous. It was, however, enlivened by a visit to the Duke of Norfolk's seat,
Greystoke. Shelley spent his last guinea on the trip;
but though the ladies of his family enjoyed the honour of
some days passed in ducal hospitalities, the visit was not
fruitful of results. The Duke at this time kindly did his
best, but without success, to bring about a reconciliation
between his old friend, the member for Horsham, and his
rebellious son.

Another important incident of the Keswick residence
was Shelley's letter to William Godwin, whose work on
Political Justice he had studied with unbounded admiration. He never spoke of this book without respect in
after-life, affirming that the perusal of it had turned his
attention from romances to questions of public utility.
The earliest letter dated to Godwin from Keswick, January
3, 1812, is in many respects remarkable, and not the least so
as a specimen of self-delineation. He entreats Godwin to
become his guide, philosopher, and friend, urging that "if
desire for universal happiness has any claim upon your
preference," if persecution and injustice suffered in the
cause of philanthropy and truth may commend a young
man to William Godwin's regard, he is not unworthy of

this honour.   We who have learned to know the flawless
purity of Shelley's aspirations, can refrain from smiling at
the big generalities of this epistle.   Words which to men
made callous by long contact with the world, ring false
and wake suspicion, were for Shelley but the natural
expression of his most abiding mood.   Yet Godwin
may be pardoned if he wished to know more in detail of
the youth, who sought to cast himself upon his care in
all the panoply of phrases about philanthropy and universal happiness.   Shelley's second letter contains an
extraordinary mixture of truth willingly communicated,
and of curious romance, illustrating his tendency to colour
facts with the hallucinations of an ardent fancy.   Of his
sincerity there is, I think, no doubt.   He really meant
what he wrote ; and yet we have no reason to believe the
statement that he was twice expelled from Eton for dis-
seminating the doctrines of *Political Justice,* or that his
father wished to drive him by poverty to accept a com-
mission in some distant regiment, in order that he might
prosecute the *Necessity of Atheism* in his absence, procure
a sentence of outlawry, and so convey the family estates to
his younger brother.   The embroidery of bare fact with a
tissue of imagination was a peculiarity of Shelley's mind ;
and this letter may be used as a key for the explanation
of many strange occurrences in his biography.   What he
tells Godwin about his want of love for his father, and his
inability to learn from the tutors imposed upon him at
Eton and Oxford, represents the simple truth.   Only from
teachers chosen by himself, and recognized as his superiors
by his own deliberate judgment, can he receive instruc-
tion.   To Godwin he resigns himself with the implicit
confidence of admiration.   Godwin was greatly struck with
this letter.   Indeed he must have been " or God or

beast," like the insensible man in Aristotle's *Ethics*, if he
could have resisted the devotion of so splendid and high-
spirited a nature, poured forth in language at once so
vehement and so convincingly sincere. He accepted the
responsible post of Shelley's Mentor; and thus began a
connexion which proved not only a source of moral
support and intellectual guidance to the poet, but was also
destined to end in a closer personal tie between the two
illustrious men.

In his second letter Shelley told Godwin that he was
then engaged in writing " An inquiry into the causes of
the failure of the French Revolution to benefit mankind,"
adding, " My plan is that of resolving to lose no oppor-
tunity to disseminate truth and happiness." Godwin
sensibly replied that Shelley was too young to set himself up as a teacher and apostle : but his pupil did not
take the hint. A third letter (Jan. 16, 1812) contains
this startling announcement : " In a few days we set off
to Dublin. I do not know exactly where, but a letter
addressed to Keswick will find me. Our journey has
been settled some time. We go principally *to forward as
much as we can* the Catholic Emancipation." In a fourth
letter (Jan. 28, 1812) he informs Godwin that he has
already prepared an address to the Catholics of Ireland, and
combats the dissuasions of his counsellor with ingenious
arguments to prove that his contemplated expedition can
do no harm, and may be fruitful of great good.

It appears that for some time past Shelley had devoted his
attention to Irish politics. The persecution of Mr. Peter
Finnerty, an Irish journalist and editor of *The Press*
newspaper, who had been sentenced to eighteen months'
imprisonment in Lincoln jail (between Feb. 7, 1811, and
Aug. 7, 1812) for plain speech about Lord Castlereagh,

roused his hottest indignation. He published a poem, as yet unrecovered, for his benefit ; the proceeds of the sale amounting, it is said, to nearly one hundred pounds.[1] The young enthusiast, who was attempting a philosophic study of the French Revolution, whose heart was glowing with universal philanthropy, and who burned to disseminate truth and happiness, judged that Ireland would be a fitting field for making a first experiment in practical politics. Armed with the MS. of his *Address to the Irish People*,[2] he set sail with Harriet and Eliza on the 3rd of February from Whitehaven. They touched the Isle of Man ; and after a very stormy passage, which drove them to the north coast of Ireland, and forced them to complete their journey by land, the party reached Dublin travelworn, but with unabated spirit, on the 12th. Harriet shared her husband's philanthropical enthusiasm. "My wife," wrote Shelley to Godwin, "is the partner of my thoughts and feelings." Indeed, there is abundant proof in both his letters and hers, about this period, that they felt and worked together. Miss Westbrook, meantime, ruled the household ; "Eliza keeps our common stock of money for safety in some nook or corner of her dress, but we are not dependent on her, although she gives it out as we want it." This master-touch of unconscious delineation tells us all we need to know about the domestic party now established in 7, Lower Sackville Street. Before a week had passed, the *Address to the Irish People* had been printed. Shelley and Harriet immediately engaged their whole energies in the task of distribution. It was advertised for sale ; but that alone seemed insufficient.

---

[1] McCarthy, p. 255.

[2] It was published in Dublin. See reprint in McCarthy, p. 179.

On the 27th of February Shelley wrote to a friend in England : "I have already sent 400 of my Irish pamphlets into the world, and they have excited a sensation of wonder in Dublin. Eleven hundred yet remain for distribution. Copies have been sent to sixty public-houses. . . . . Expectation is on the tiptoe. I send a man out every day to distribute copies, with instructions where and how to give them. His account corresponds with the multitudes of people who possess them. I stand at the balcony of our window and watch till I see a man *who looks likely.* I throw a book to him."

A postscript to this letter lets us see the propaganda from Harriet's point of view. "I am sure you would laugh were you to see us give the pamphlets. We throw them out of window, and give them to men that we pass in the streets. For myself, I am ready to die of laughter when it is done, and Percy looks so grave. Yesterday he put one into a woman's hood of a cloak."

The purpose of this address was to rouse the Irish people to a sense of their real misery, to point out that Catholic Emancipation and a Repeal of the Union Act were the only radical remedies for their wrongs, and to teach them the spirit in which they should attempt a revolution. On the last point Shelley felt intensely. The whole address aims at the inculcation of a noble moral temper, tolerant, peaceful, resolute, rational, and self-denying. Considered as a treatise on the principles which should govern patriots during a great national crisis, the document is admirable : and if the inhabitants of Dublin had been a population of Shelleys, its effect might have been permanent and overwhelming. The mistake lay in supposing that a people whom the poet himself described as " of scarcely greater elevation in the scale of intellectual

being than the oyster," were qualified to take the remedy
of their grievances into their own hands, or were amenable
to such sound reasoning as he poured forth. He told
Godwin that he had "wilfully vulgarized the language of
this pamphlet, in order to reduce the remarks it contains
to the taste and comprehension of the Irish peasantry."
A few extracts will enable the reader to judge how far he
had succeeded in this aim. I select such as seem to me
most valuable for the light they throw upon his own
opinions. "All religions are good which make men good;
and the way that a person ought to prove that his method
of worshipping God is best, is for himself to be better
than all other men." "A Protestant is my brother, and
a Catholic is my brother." "Do not inquire if a man be
a heretic, if he be a Quaker, a Jew, or a heathen ; but if
he be a virtuous man, if he loves liberty and truth, if he
wish the happiness and peace of human kind. If a man
be ever so much a believer and love not these things, he
is a heartless hypocrite, a rascal, and a knave." "It is
not a merit to tolerate, but it is a crime to be intolerant."
"Anything short of unlimited toleration and complete
charity with all men, on which you will recollect that
Jesus Christ principally insisted, is wrong." "Be calm,
mild, deliberate, patient. . . . . Think and talk and
discuss. . . . . Be free and be happy, but first be wise
and good." Proceeding to recommend the formation of
associations, he condemns secret and violent societies ;
"Be fair, open, and you will be terrible to your enemies."
"Habits of SOBRIETY, REGULARITY, and THOUGHT must
be entered into and firmly resolved upon." Then follow
precepts, which Shelley no doubt regarded as practical,
for the purification of private morals, and the regulation
of public discussion by the masses whom he elsewhere

recognized as "thousands huddled together, one mass of animated filth."

The foregoing extracts show that Shelley was in no sense an inflammatory demagogue ; however visionary may have been the hopes he indulged, he based those hopes upon the still more Utopian foundation of a sudden ethical reform, and preached a revolution without blood-shed. We find in them, moreover, the germs of *The Revolt of Islam,* where the hero plays the part successfully in fiction, which the poet had attempted without appre-ciable result in practice at Dublin. The same principles guided Shelley at a still later period. When he wrote his *Masque of Anarchy,* he bade the people of England to assemble by thousands, strong in the truth and justice of their cause, invincible in peaceful opposition to force.

While he was sowing his Address broadcast in the streets of Dublin, Shelley was engaged in printing a second pamphlet on the subject of Catholic Emancipation. It was entitled *Proposals for an Association,* and advocated in serious and temperate phrase the formation of a vast society, binding all the Catholic patriots of Ireland together, for the recovery of their rights. In estimating Shelley's political sagacity, it must be remembered that Catholic Emancipation has since his day been brought about by the very measure he proposed and under the conditions he foresaw. Speaking of the English Govern-ment in his Address, he used these simple phrases :—" It wants altering and mending. It will be mended, and a reform of English Government will produce good to the Irish." These sentences were prophetic ; and perhaps they are destined to be even more so.

With a view to presenting at one glance Shelley's posi-tion as a practical politician, I shall anticipate the course of a few years, and compare his Irish pamphlets with an essay published in 1817, under the title of *A Proposal for putting Reform to the Vote throughout the Kingdom.* He saw that the House of Commons did not represent the country ; and acting upon his principle that government is the servant of the governed, he sought means for ascertaining the real will of the nation with regard to its Parliament, and for bringing the collective opinion of the population to bear upon its rulers. The plan proposed was that a huge network of committees should be formed, and that by their means every individual man should be canvassed. We find here the same method of advancing reform by peaceable associations as in Ireland. How moderate were his own opinions with regard to the franchise, is proved by the following sentence :—" With respect to Universal Suffrage, I confess I consider its adoption, in the present unprepared state of public knowledge and feeling, a measure fraught with peril. I think that none but those who register their names as paying a certain small sum in *direct taxes* ought at present to send members to Parliament." As in the case of Ireland, so in that of England, subsequent events have shown that Shelley's hopes were not exaggerated.

While the Shelleys were in Dublin, a meeting of the Irish Catholics was announced for the evening of Feb. 28. It was held in Fishamble Street Theatre ; and here Shelley made his *début* as an orator. He spoke for about an hour ; and his speech was, on the whole, well received, though it raised some hisses at the beginning by his remarks upon Roman Catholicism. There is no proof that Shelley, though eloquent in conversation, was a powerful public speaker. The somewhat conflicting accounts we have received of this, his maiden effort, tend to the im-

pression that he failed to carry his audience with him.
The dissemination of his pamphlets had, however, raised
considerable interest in his favour; and he was welcomed
by the press as an Englishman of birth and fortune, who
wished well to the Irish cause.   His youth told somewhat
against him.   It was difficult to take the strong words of
the beardless boy at their real value; and as though to
aggravate this drawback, his Irish servant, Daniel Hill, an
efficient agent in the dissemination of the Address, affirmed
that his master was fifteen—four years less than his real
age.

In Dublin Shelley made acquaintance with Curran,
whose jokes and dirty stories he could not appreciate, and
with a Mr. Lawless, who began a history of the Irish
people in concert with the young philosopher.   We also
obtain, from one of Harriet's letters, a somewhat humorous
peep at another of their friends, a patriotic Mrs. Nugent,
who supported herself by working in a furrier's shop, and
who is described as "sitting in the room now, and talking
to Percy about Virtue."   After less than two months' experience of his Irish propaganda, Shelley came to the
conclusion that he "had done all that he could."   The
population of Dublin had not risen to the appeal of their
Laon with the rapidity he hoped for; and accordingly
upon the 7th of April he once more embarked with his
family for Holyhead.   In after-days he used to hint that
the police had given him warning that it would be well for
him to leave Dublin; but, though the danger of a prosecu-
tion was not wholly visionary, this intimation does not seem
to have been made.   Before he quitted Ireland, however, he
despatched a box containing the remaining copies of his
Address and *Proposals*, together with the recently printed
edition of another manifesto, called a *Declaration of*

Rights, to a friend in Sussex. This box was delayed at
the Holyhead custom-house, and opened. Its contents gave
serious anxiety to the Surveyor of Customs, who communicated the astonishing discovery through the proper
official channels to the government. After some correspondence, the authorities decided to take no steps against
Shelley, and the box was forwarded to its destination.

The friend in question was a Miss Eliza Hitchener, of
Hurstpierpoint, who kept a sort of school, and who had
attracted Shelley's favourable notice by her advanced
political and religious opinions. He does not seem to have
made her personal acquaintance ; but some of his most
interesting letters from Ireland are addressed to her.
How recklessly he entered into serious entanglements with
people whom he had not learned to know, may be gathered
from these extracts :—"We will meet you in Wales, and
never part again. It will not do. In compliance
with Harriet's earnest solicitations, I entreated you
instantly to come and join our circle, resign your school,
all, everything for us and the Irish cause." "I ought to
count myself a favoured mortal with such a wife and such
a friend." Harriet addressed this lady as "Portia ;" and
it is an undoubted fact that soon after their return to
England, Miss Hitchener formed one of their permanent
family circle. Her entrance into it and her exit from it
at no very distant period are, however, both obscure.
Before long she acquired another name than Portia in the
Shelley household, and now she is better known to fame
as the "Brown Demon." Eliza Westbrook took a strong
dislike to her ; Harriet followed suit ; and Shelley himself
found that he had liked her better at a distance than in
close companionship. She had at last to be bought off or
bribed to leave.

F

The scene now shifts with bewildering frequency ; nor
is it easy to trace the Shelleys in their rapid flight.
About the 21st of April, they settled for a short time at
Nantgwilt, near Rhayader, in North Wales. Ere long we
find them at Lynmouth on the Somersetshire coast. Here
Shelley continued his political propaganda, by circulating
the *Declaration of Rights*, whereof mention has already
been made. It was, as Mr. W. M. Rossetti first pointed
out, a manifesto concerning the ends of government and
the rights of man,—framed in imitation of two similar
French Revolutionary documents, issued by the Con-
stituent Assembly in August, 1789, and by Robespierre
in April, 1793.[1] Shelley used to seal this pamphlet in
bottles and set it afloat upon the sea, hoping perhaps that
after this wise it would traverse St. George's Channel and
reach the sacred soil of Erin. He also employed his
servant, Daniel Hill, to distribute it among the Somersetshire farmers. On the 19th of August this man was
arrested in the streets of Barnstaple, and sentenced to six
months' imprisonment for uttering a seditious pamphlet ;
and the remaining copies of the *Declaration of Rights*
were destroyed. In strong contrast with the puerility of
these proceedings, is the grave and lofty *Letter to Lord
Ellenborough*, composed at Lynmouth, and printed at
Barnstaple.[2] A printer, named D. J. Eaton, had recently
been sentenced to imprisonment by his Lordship for pub-
lishing the Third Part of Paine's *Age of Reason*. Shelley's
epistle is an eloquent argument in favour of toleration and
the freedom of the intellect, carrying the matter beyond
the instance of legal tyranny which occasioned its compo-

---

[1] Reprinted in McCarthy, p. 324.
[2] Reprinted in Lady Shelley's Memorials, p. 29.

sition, and treating it with philosophic, if impassioned
seriousness.

An extract from this composition will serve to show his
power of handling weighty English prose, while yet a
youth of hardly twenty. I have chosen a passage
bearing on his theological opinions :—

> Moral qualities are such as only a human being can possess.
> To attribute them to the Spirit of the Universe, or to suppose that
> it is capable of altering them, is to degrade God into man, and to
> annex to this incomprehensible Being qualities incompatible with
> any possible definition of his nature.
>
> It may be here objected : Ought not the Creator to possess the
> perfections of the creature ? No. To attribute to God the moral
> qualities of man, is to suppose him susceptible of passions, which
> arising out of corporeal organization, it is plain that a pure spirit
> cannot possess. . . . But even suppose, with the vulgar, that God
> is a venerable old man, seated on a throne of clouds, his breast
> the theatre of various passions, analogous to those of humanity,
> his will changeable and uncertain as that of an earthly king ;
> still, goodness and justice are qualities seldom nominally denied
> him, and it will be admitted that he disapproves of any action
> incompatible with those qualities. Persecution for opinion is
> unjust. With what consistency, then, can the worshippers of a
> Deity whose benevolence they boast, embitter the existence of
> their fellow-being, because his ideas of that Deity are different
> from those which they entertain ? Alas ! there is no consistency
> in those persecutors who worship a benevolent Deity ; those who
> worship a demon would alone act consonantly to these principles
> by imprisoning and torturing in his name.

Shelley had more than once urged Godwin and his
family to visit him. The sage of Skinner Street thought
that now was a convenient season. Accordingly he left
London, and travelled by coach to Lynmouth, where he
found that the Shelleys had flitted a few days previously
without giving any notice. This fruitless journey of the
poet's Mentor is humorously described by Hogg, as well
as one undertaken by himself in the following year to

Dublin with a similar result. The Shelleys were now
established at Tan-yr-allt, near Tremadoc, in North Wales,
on an estate belonging to Mr. W. A. Madocks, M.P. for
Boston. This gentleman had reclaimed a considerable
extent of marshy ground from the sea, and protected it
with an embankment. Shelley, whose interest in the
poor people around him was always keen and practical,
lost no time in making their acquaintance at Tremadoc.
The work of utility carried out by his landlord aroused
his enthusiastic admiration ; and when the embankment
was emperilled by a heavy sea, he got up a subscription
for its preservation. Heading the list with 500*l.*, how
raised, or whether paid, we know not, he endeavoured to
extract similar sums from the neighbouring gentry, and
even ran up with Harriet to London to use his influence
for the same purpose with the Duke of Norfolk. On
this occasion he made the personal acquaintance of the
Godwin family.

Life at Tanyrallt was smooth and studious, except for
the diversion caused by the peril to the embankment.
We hear of Harriet continuing her Latin studies, reading
Odes of Horace, and projecting an epistle in that language
to Hogg. Shelley, as usual, collected many books around
him. There are letters extant in which he writes to
London for Spinoza and Kant, Plato, and the works of
the chief Greek historians. It appears that at this period,
under the influence of Godwin, he attempted to conquer a
strong natural dislike for history. "I am determined to
apply myself to a study which is hateful and disgusting to
my very soul, but which is above all studies necessary for
him who would be listened to as a mender of antiquated
abuses,—I mean, that record of crimes and miseries—
history." Although he may have made an effort to apply

himself to historical reading, he was not successful. His true bias inclined him to metaphysics coloured by a glowing fancy, and to poetry penetrated with speculative enthusiasm. In the historic sense he was deficient; and when he made a serious effort at a later period to compose a tragedy upon the death of Charles I., this work was taken up with reluctance, continued with effort, and finally abandoned.

In the same letters he speaks about a collection of short poems on which he was engaged, and makes frequent allusions to *Queen Mab*. It appears from his own assertion, and from Medwin's biography, that a poem on Queen Mab had been projected and partially written by him at the early age of eighteen. But it was not taken seriously in hand until the spring of 1812; nor was it finished and printed before 1813. The first impression was a private issue of 250 copies, on fine paper, which Shelley distributed to people whom he wished to influence. It was pirated soon after its appearance, and again in 1821 it was given to the public by a bookseller named Clarke. Against the latter republication Shelley energetically protested, disclaiming in a letter addressed to *The Examiner*, from Pisa, June 22, 1821, any interest in a production which he had not even seen for several years. "I doubt not but that it is perfectly worthless in point of literary composition; and that in all that concerns moral and political speculation, as well as in the subtler discriminations of metaphysical and religious doctrine, it is still more crude and immature. I am a devoted enemy to religious, political, and domestic oppression; and I regret this publication, not so much from literary vanity as because I fear it is better fitted to injure than to serve the sacred cause of freedom." This judgment is undoubtedly severe ; but, though exaggerated in its condemnation, it, like all Shelley's criticisms on his own works, expresses the truth. We cannot include *Queen Mab*, in spite of its sonorous rhetoric and fervid declamation, in the canon of his masterpieces. It had a *succès de scandale* on its first appearance, and fatally injured Shelley's reputation. As a work of art it lacks maturity and permanent vitality.

The Shelleys were suddenly driven away from Tany-rallt by a mysterious occurrence, of which no satisfactory explanation has yet been given. According to letters written by himself and Harriet soon after the event, and confirmed by the testimony of Eliza, Shelley was twice attacked upon the night of Feb. 24, by an armed ruffian, with whom he struggled in a hand-to-hand combat. Pistols were fired and windows broken, and Shelley's nightgown was shot through: but the assassin made his escape from the house without being recognized. His motive and his personality still remain matters of conjecture. Whether the whole affair was a figment of Shelley's brain, rendered more than usually susceptible by laudanum taken to assuage intense physical pain; whether it was a perilous hoax played upon him by the Irish servant, Daniel Hill ; or whether, as he himself surmised, the crime was instigated by an unfriendly neighbour, it is impossible to say. Strange adventures of this kind, blending fact and fancy in a now inextricable tangle, are of no unfrequent occurrence in Shelley's biography. In estimating the relative proportions of the two factors in this case, it must be borne in mind, on the one hand, that no one but Shelley, who was alone in the parlour, and who for some unexplained reason had loaded his pistols on the evening before the alleged assault, professed to have seen

the villain ; and, on the other, that the details furnished
by Harriet, and confirmed at a subsequent period by so
hostile a witness as Eliza, are too circumstantial to be lightly
set aside.

On the whole it appears most probable that Shelley on
this night was the subject of a powerful hallucination.
The theory of his enemies at Tanyrallt, that the story had
been invented to facilitate his escape from the neighbourhood without paying his bills, may be dismissed.   But
no investigation on the spot could throw any clear light on
the circumstance, and Shelley's friends, Hogg, Peacock,
and Mr. Madocks, concurred in regarding the affair as a
delusion.

There was no money in the common purse of the
Shelleys at this moment.   In their distress they applied
to Mr. T. Hookham, a London publisher, who sent them
enough to carry them across the Irish Channel.   After a
short residence in 35, Cuffe Street, Dublin, and a flying
visit to Killarney, they returned to London.   Eliza, for
some reason as unexplained as the whole episode of this
second visit to Ireland, was left behind for a short season.
The flight from Tanyrallt closes the first important period
of Shelley's life ; and his settlement in London marks the
beginning of another, fruitful of the gravest consequences
and decisive for his future.

CHAPTER IV.

SECOND RESIDENCE IN LONDON, AND SEPARATION FROM
HARRIET.

EARLY in May the Shelleys arrived in London, where
they were soon joined by Eliza, from whose increasingly
irksome companionship the poet had recently enjoyed a
few weeks' respite.   After living for a short while in hotels,
they took lodgings in Half Moon Street.   The house had
a projecting window, where the poet loved to sit with book
in hand, and catch, according to his custom, the maximum
of sunlight granted by a chary English summer.   "He
wanted," said one of his female admirers, "only a pan of
clear water and a fresh turf to look like some young lady's
lark, hanging outside for air and song."   According to
Hogg, this period of London life was a pleasant and tranquil episode in Shelley's troubled career.   His room was
full of books, among which works of German metaphysics
occupied a prominent place, though they were not deeply
studied.   He was now learning Italian, and made his first
acquaintance with Tasso, Ariosto, and Petrarch.

The habits of the household were, to say the least,
irregular; for Shelley took no thought of sublunary
matters, and Harriet was an indifferent housekeeper.
Dinner seems to have come to them less by forethought
than by the operation of divine chance; and when there

was no meat provided for the entertainment of casual guests, the table was supplied with buns, procured by Shelley from the nearest pastry-cook. He had already abjured animal food and alcohol ; and his favourite diet consisted of pulse or bread, which he ate dry with water, or made into panada. Hogg relates how, when he was walking in the streets and felt hungry, he would dive into a baker's shop and emerge with a loaf tucked under his arm. This he consumed as he went along, very often reading at the same time, and dodging the foot-passengers with the rapidity of movement which distinguished him. He could not comprehend how any man should want more than bread. "I have dropped a word, a hint," says Hogg, "about a pudding ; a pudding, Bysshe said dogmatically, is a prejudice." This indifference to diet was highly characteristic of Shelley. During the last years of his life, even when he was suffering from the frequent attacks of a painful disorder, he took no heed of food ; and his friend, Trelawny, attributes the derangement of his health, in a great measure, to this carelessness. Mrs. Shelley used to send him something to eat into the room where he habitually studied ; but the plate frequently remained untouched for hours upon a bookshelf, and at the end of the day he might be heard asking, "Mary, have I dined ? " His dress was no less simple than his diet. Hogg says that he never saw him in a great coat, and that his collar was unbuttoned to let the air play freely on his throat. "In the street or road he reluctantly wore a hat ; but in fields and gardens, his little round head had no other covering than his long, wild, ragged locks." Shelley's head, as is well known, was remarkably small and round ; he used to plunge it several times a day in cold water, and expose it recklessly to the intensest heat of fire or sun.

Mrs. Shelley relates that a great part of the *Cenci* was written on their house-roof near Leghorn, where Shelley lay exposed to the unmitigated ardour of Italian summer heat; and Hogg describes him reading Homer by a blazing fire-light, or roasting his skull upon the hearth-rug by the hour.

These personal details cannot be omitted by the biographer of such a man as Shelley. He was an elemental and primeval creature, as little subject to the laws of custom in his habits as in his modes of thought, living literally as the spirit moved him, with a natural nonchalance that has perhaps been never surpassed. To time and place he was equally indifferent, and could not be got to remember his engagements. " He took strange caprices, unfounded frights and dislikes, vain apprehensions and panic terrors, and therefore he absented himself from formal and sacred engagements. He was unconscious and oblivious of times, places, persons, and seasons; and falling into some poetic vision, some day-dream, he quickly and completely forgot all that he had repeatedly and solemnly promised; or he ran away after some object of imaginary urgency and importance, which suddenly came into his head, setting off in vain pursuit of it, he knew not whither. When he was caught, brought up in custody, and turned over to the ladies, with, Behold, your King! to be caressed, courted, admired, and flattered, the king of beauty and fancy would too commonly bolt; slip away, steal out, creep off; unobserved and almost magically he vanished; thus mysteriously depriving his fair subjects of his much-coveted, long looked-for company." If he had been fairly caged and found himself in congenial company, he let time pass unheeded, sitting up all night to talk, and chaining his audience by the spell of his unri-

valled eloquence ; for wonderful as was his poetry, those
who enjoyed the privilege of converse with him, judged
it even more attractive. " He was commonly most com-
municative, unreserved, and éloquent, and enthusiastic,
when those around him were inclining to yield to the
influence of sleep, or rather at the hour when they would
have been disposed to seek their chambers, but for the
bewitching charms of his discourse."

From Half Moon Street the Shelleys moved into a
house in Pimlico ; and it was here according to Hogg, or
at Cooke's Hotel in Dover Street according to other
accounts, that Shelley's first child, Ianthe Eliza, was born
about the end of June, 1813.   Harriet did not take much to
her little girl, and gave her over to a wet-nurse, for whom
Shelley conceived a great dislike.   That a mother should
not nurse her own baby was no doubt contrary to his
principles; and the double presence of the servant and
Eliza, whom he now most cordially detested, made his
home uncomfortable.   We have it on excellent authority,
that of Mr. Peacock, that he " was extremely fond of it
(the child), and would walk up and down a room with it
in his arms for a long time together, singing to it a song
of his own making, which ran on the repetition of a word
of his own coining.   His song was Yáhmani, Yáhmani,
Yáhmani, Yáhmani."   To the want of sympathy between
the father and the mother in this matter of Ianthe, Mr.
Peacock is inclined to attribute the beginning of troubles
in the Shelley household.   There is, indeed, no doubt
that the revelation of Harriet's maternal coldness must
have been extremely painful to her husband ; and how far
she carried her insensibility, may be gathered from a story
told by Hogg about her conduct during an operation performed upon the child.

During this period of his sojourn in London, Shelley was again in some pecuniary difficulties. Yet he indulged Harriet's vanity by setting up a carriage, in which they afterwards took a hurried journey to Edinburgh and back. He narrowly escaped a debtor's prison through this act of extravagance, and by a somewhat ludicrous mistake Hogg was arrested for the debt due to the coachmaker. His acquaintances were few and scattered, and he saw nothing of his family. Gradually, however, he seems to have become a kind of prophet in a coterie of learned ladies. The views he had propounded in *Queen Mab*, his passionate belief in the perfectibility of man, his vegetarian doctrines, and his readiness to adopt any new nostrum for the amelioration of the race, endeared him to all manners of strange people; nor was he deterred by aristocratic prejudices from frequenting society which proved extremely uncongenial to Hogg, and of which we have accordingly some caustic sketches from his pen. His chief friends were a Mrs. Boinville, for whom he conceived an enthusiastic admiration, and her daughter Cornelia, married to a vegetarian, Mr. Newton. In order to be near them he had moved to Pimlico; and his next move, from London to a cottage named High Elms, at Bracknell, in Berkshire, had the same object. With Godwin and his family he was also on terms of familiar intercourse. Under the philosopher's roof in Skinner Street there was now gathered a group of miscellaneous inmates— Fanny Imlay, the daughter of his first wife, Mary Wollstonecraft; Mary, his own daughter by the same marriage; his second wife, and her two children, Claire and Charles Clairmont, the offspring of a previous union. From this connexion with the Godwin household events of the gravest importance in the future were destined to arise, and already it appears

that Fanny Imlay had begun to look with perilous approval
on the fascinating poet. Hogg and Mr. Peacock, the
well-known novelist, described by Mrs. Newton as "a
cold scholar, who, I think, has neither taste nor feeling,"
were his only other intimates.

Mrs. Newton's unfair judgment of Mr. Peacock
marks a discord between the two chief elements of
Shelley's present society ; and indeed it will appear to a
careful student of his biography that Hogg, Peacock,
and Harriet, now stood somewhat by themselves and
aloof from the inner circle of his associates. If we
regard the Shelleys as the centre of an extended line,
we shall find the Westbrook family at one end, the Boinville family at the other, with Hogg and Peacock some-
where in the middle. Harriet was naturally drawn to the
Westbrook extremity, and Shelley to the Boinville.
Peacock had no affinity for either, but a sincere regard for
Harriet as well as for her husband ; while Hogg was in
much the same position, except that he had made friends
with Mrs. Newton. The Godwins, of great importance to
Shelley himself, exercised their influence at a distance
from the rest. Frequent change from Bracknell to London
and back again, varied by the flying journey to Edinburgh,
and a last visit paid in strictest secrecy to his mother and
sisters, at Field Place, of which a very interesting record
is left in the narrative of Mr. Kennedy, occupied the
interval between July, 1813, and March, 1814. The
period was not productive of literary masterpieces. We
only hear of a *Refutation of Deism*, a dialogue between
Eusebes and Theosophus, which attacked all forms of
Theistic belief.

Since we are now approaching the gravest crisis in
Shelley's life, it behoves us to be more than usually

careful in considering his circumstances at this epoch.
His home had become cold and dull. Harriet did not love
her child, and spent her time in a great measure with her
Mount Street relations. Eliza was a source of continual
irritation, and the Westbrook family did its best, by
interference and suggestion, to refrigerate the poet's feelings
for his wife. On the other hand he found among the Boinville set exactly that high-flown, enthusiastic, sentimental
atmosphere which suited his idealizing temper. Two
extracts from a letter written to Hogg upon the 16th of
March, 1814, speak more eloquently than any analysis,
and will place before the reader the antagonism which
had sprung up in Shelley's mind between his own home
and the circle of his new friends :—" I have been staying
with Mrs. B—— for the last month ; I have escaped, in
the society of all that philosophy and friendship combine,
from the dismaying solitude of myself. They have
revived in my heart the expiring flame of life. I have
felt myself translated to a paradise, which has nothing of
mortality but its transitoriness ; my heart sickens at the
view of that necessity, which will quickly divide me from
the delightful tranquillity of this happy home,—for it has
become my home. The trees, the bridge, the minutest
objects, have already a place in my affections."

" Eliza is still with us,—not here !—but will be with
me when the infinite malice of destiny forces me to
depart. I am now but little inclined to contest this point.
I certainly hate her with all my heart and soul. It is a
sight which awakens an inexpressible sensation of disgust
and horror, to see her caress my poor little Ianthe, in whom
I may hereafter find the consolation of sympathy. I sometimes feel faint with the fatigue of checking the overflow-
ings of my unbounded abhorrence for this miserable

wretch. But she is no more than a blind and loathsome worm, that cannot see to sting."

While divided in this way between a home which had become distasteful to him, and a house where he found scope for his most romantic outpourings of sensibility, Shelley fell suddenly and passionately in love with Godwin's daughter, Mary. Peacock, who lived in close intimacy with him at this period, must deliver his testimony as to the overwhelming nature of the new attachment :—" Nothing that I ever read in tale or history could present a more striking image of a sudden, violent, irresistible, uncontrollable passion, than that under which I found him labouring when, at his request, I went up from the country to call on him in London. Between his old feelings towards Harriet, *from whom he was not then separated*, and his new passion for Mary, he showed in his looks, in his gestures, in his speech, the state of a mind ' suffering, like a little kingdom, the nature of an insurrection.' His eyes were bloodshot, his hair and dress disordered. He caught up a bottle of laudanum, and said, ' I never part from this.' "

We may therefore affirm, I think, with confidence that in the winter and spring of 1814, Shelley had been becoming gradually more and more estranged from Harriet, whose commonplace nature was no mate for his, and whom he had never loved with all the depth of his affection ; that his intimacy with the Boinville family had brought into painful prominence whatever was jarring and repugnant to him in his home ; and that in this crisis of his fate he had fallen in love for the first time seriously with Mary Godwin.[1] She was then a girl of sixteen, "fair and fair-

[1] The date at which he first made Mary's acquaintance is uncertain. Peacock says that it was between April 18 and June 8.

haired, pale indeed, and with a piercing look," to quote
Hogg's description of her, as she first appeared before him
on the 8th or 9th of June, 1814. With her freedom from
prejudice, her tense and high-wrought sensibility, her
acute intellect, enthusiasm for ideas, and vivid imagination, Mary Godwin was naturally a fitter companion for
Shelley than the good Harriet, however beautiful.

That Shelley early in 1814 had no intention of leaving
his wife, is probable; for he was re-married to her on the
24th of March, eight days after his impassioned letter to
Hogg, in St. George's, Hanover Square. Harriet was
pregnant, and this ratification of the Scotch marriage was
no doubt intended to place the legitimacy of a possible
heir beyond all question. Yet it seems, if we may found
conjecture on "Stanzas, April, 1814," that in the very
month after this new ceremony Shelley found the
difficulties of his wedded life insuperable, and that he was
already making up his mind to part from Harriet. About
the middle of June the separation actually occurred—not
by mutual consent, so far as any published documents
throw light upon the matter, but rather by Shelley's
sudden abandonment of his wife and child.[1] For a short
while Harriet was left in ignorance of his abode, and with
a very insufficient sum of money at her disposal. She
placed herself under the protection of her father, retired
to Bath, and about the beginning of July received a letter
from Shelley, who was thenceforth solicitous for her wel-
fare, keeping up a correspondence with her, supplying her
with funds, and by no means shrinking from personal
communications.

---

[1] Leigh Hunt, Autob. p. 236, and Medwin, however, both assert
that it was by mutual consent. The whole question must be
studied in Peacock and in Garnett, Relics of Shelley, p. 147.

That Shelley must bear the responsibility of this separation seems to me quite clear. His justification is to be found in his avowed opinions on the subject of love and marriage—opinions which Harriet knew well and professed to share, and of which he had recently made ample confession in the notes to *Queen Mab*. The world will still agree with Lord Eldon in regarding those opinions as dangerous to society, and a blot upon the poet's character; but it would be unfair, while condemning them as frankly as he professed them, to blame him also because he did not conform to the opposite code of morals, for which he frequently expressed extreme abhorrence, and which he stigmatized, however wrongly, as the source of the worst social vices. It must be added that the Shelley family in their memorials of the poet, and through their friend, Mr. Richard Garnett, inform us, without casting any slur on Harriet, that documents are extant which will completely vindicate the poet's conduct in this matter. It is therefore but just to await their publication before pronouncing a decided judgment. Meanwhile there remains no doubt about the fact that forty days after leaving Harriet, Shelley departed from London with Mary Godwin, who had consented to share his fortunes. How he plighted his new troth, and won the hand of her who was destined to be his companion for life, may best be told in Lady Shelley's words :—

"His anguish, his isolation, his difference from other men, his gifts of genius and eloquent enthusiasm, made a deep impression on Godwin's daughter Mary, now a girl of sixteen, who had been accustomed to hear Shelley spoken of as something rare and strange. To her, as they met one eventful day in St. Pancras Churchyard, by her mother's grave, Bysshe, in burning words, poured forth the tale of

G

his wild past—how he had suffered, how he had been
misled, and how, if supported by her love, he hoped in
future years to enrol his name with the wise and good who
had done battle for their fellow-men, and been true through
all adverse storms to the cause of humanity. Unhesitat-
ingly, she placed her hand in his, and linked her fortune
with his own; and most truthfully, as the remaining portions of these Memorials will prove, was the pledge of both
redeemed. The theories in which the daughter of the
authors of *Political Justice,* and of the *Rights of Woman,*
had been educated, spared her from any conflict between
her duty and her affection. For she was the child of
parents whose writings had had for their object to prove
that marriage was one among the many institutions which
a new era in the history of mankind was about to sweep
away. By her father, whom she loved—by the writings
of her mother, whom she had been taught to venerate—
these doctrines had been rendered familiar to her mind.
It was therefore natural that she should listen to the dic-
tates of her own heart, and willingly unite her fate with
one who was so worthy of her love."

Soon after her withdrawal to Bath, Harriet gave birth
to Shelley's second child, Charles Bysshe, who died in
1826. She subsequently formed another connexion which
proved unhappy; and on the 10th of November, 1816,
she committed suicide by drowning herself in the Serpen-
tine. The distance of time between June, 1814, and
November, 1816, and the new ties formed by Harriet in
this interval, prove that there was no immediate connexion
between Shelley's abandonment of his wife and her suicide.
She had always entertained the thought of self-destruction,
as Hogg, who is no adverse witness in her case, has amply
recorded; and it may be permitted us to suppose that,

finding herself for the second time unhappy in her love, she reverted to a long-since cherished scheme, and cut the knot of life and all its troubles.

So far as this is possible, I have attempted to narrate the most painful episode in Shelley's life as it occurred, without extenuation and without condemnation. Until the papers, mentioned with such insistence by Lady Shelley and Mr. Garnett, are given to the world, it is impossible that the poet should not bear the reproach of heartlessness and inconstancy in this the gravest of all human relations. Such, however, is my belief in the essential goodness of his character, after allowing, as we must do, for the operation of his peculiar principles upon his conduct, that I for my own part am willing to suspend my judgment till the time arrives for his vindication. The language used by Lady Shelley and Mr. Garnett justify us in expecting that that vindication will be as startling as complete. If it is not, they, as pleading for him, will have overshot the mark of prudence.

On the 28th of July Shelley left London with Mary Godwin, who up to this date had remained beneath her father's roof. There was some secrecy in their departure, because they were accompanied by Miss Clairmont, whose mother disapproved of her forming a third in the party. Having made their way to Dover, they crossed the Channel in an open boat, and went at once to Paris. Here they hired a donkey for their luggage, intending to perform the journey across France on foot. Shelley, however, sprained his ancle, and a mule-carriage was provided for the party. In this conveyance they reached the Jura, and entered Switzerland at Neufchatel. Brunnen, on the Lake of Lucerne, was chosen for their residence; and here Shelley began his romantic tale of *The Assassins*,

a portion of which is printed in his prose works. Want
of money compelled them soon to think of turning their
steps homeward; and the back journey was performed
upon the Reuss and Rhine. They reached Gravesend,
after a bad passage, on the 13th of September. Mrs.
Shelley's *History of a Six Weeks' Tour* relates the details
of this trip, which was of great importance in forming
Shelley's taste and in supplying him with the scenery of
river, rock, and mountain, so splendidly utilized in
Alastor.

The autumn was a period of more than usual money
difficulty; but on the 6th of January, 1815, Sir Bysshe
died, Percy became the next heir to the baronetcy and
the family estates, and an arrangement was made with
his father by right of which he received an allowance of
1000*l.* a year. A portion of his income was immediately
set apart for Harriet. The winter was passed in London,
where Shelley walked a hospital, in order, it is said, to
acquire some medical knowledge that might be of service
to the poor he visited. His own health at this period
was very bad. A physician whom he consulted, pronounced that he was rapidly sinking under pulmonary
disease, and he suffered frequent attacks of acute pain.
The consumptive symptoms seem to have been so marked
that for the next three years he had no doubt that he
was destined to an early death. In 1818, however, all
danger of phthisis passed away; and during the rest of
his short life he only suffered from spasms and violent
pains in the side, which baffled the physicians, but,
though they caused him extreme anguish, did not
menace any vital organ. To the subject of his health
it will be necessary to return at a later period of his
biography. For the present it is enough to remember

that his physical condition was such as to justify his own expectation of death at no distant time.[1]

Fond as ever of wandering, Shelley set out in the early summer for a tour with Mary. They visited Devonshire and Clifton, and then settled in a house on Bishopsgate Heath, near Windsor Forest. The summer was further broken by a water excursion up the Thames to its source, in the company of Mr. Peacock and Charles Clairmont. Peacock traces the poet's taste for boating, which afterwards became a passion with him, to this excursion. About this there is, however, some doubt. Medwin tells us that Shelley while a boy delighted in being on the water, and that he enjoyed the pastime at Eton. On the other hand, Mr. W. S. Halliday, a far better authority than Medwin, asserts positively that he never saw Shelley on the river at Eton, and Hogg relates nothing to prove that he practised rowing at Oxford. It is certain that, though inordinately fond of boats and every kind of water—river, sea, lake, or canal—he never learned to swim. Peacock also notices his habit of floating paper boats, and gives an amusing description of the boredom suffered by Hogg on occasions when Shelley would stop by the side of pond or mere to float a mimic navy. The not altogether apocryphal story of his having once constructed a boat out of a bank-post-bill, and launched it on the lake in Kensington Gardens, deserves to be alluded to in this connexion.

On their return from this river journey, Shelley began the poem of *Alastor*, haunting the woodland glades and oak groves of Windsor Forest, and drawing from that noble scenery his inspiration. It was printed with a few other poems in one volume the next year. Not only was

[1] See Letter to Godwin in Shelley Memorials, p. 78.

Alastor the first serious poem published by Shelley ; but it was also the first of his compositions which revealed the greatness of his genius. Rarely has blank verse been written with more majesty and music : and while the influence of Milton and Wordsworth may be traced in certain passages, the versification, tremulous with lyrical vibrations, is such as only Shelley could have produced.

"Alastor" is the Greek name for a vengeful dæmon, driving its victim into desert places ; and Shelley, prompted by Peacock, chose it for the title of a poem which describes the Nemesis of solitary souls. Apart from its intrinsic merit as a work of art, *Alastor* has great autobiographical value. Mrs. Shelley affirms that it was written under the expectation of speedy death, and under the sense of disappointment, consequent upon the misfortunes of his early life. This accounts for the somewhat unhealthy vein of sentiment which threads the wilderness of its sublime descriptions. All that Shelley had observed of natural beauty—in Wales, at Lynton, in Switzerland, upon the eddies of the Reuss, beneath the oak shades of the forest—is presented to us in a series of pictures penetrated with profound emotion. But the deeper meaning of *Alastor* is to be found, not in the thought of death nor in the poet's recent communings with nature, but in the motto from St. Augustine placed upon its title-page, and in the *Hymn to Intellectual Beauty*, composed about a year later. Enamoured of ideal loveliness, the poet pursues his vision through the universe, vainly hoping to assuage the thirst which has been stimulated in his spirit, and vainly longing for some mortal realization of his love. *Alastor*, like *Epipsychidion*, reveals the mistake which Shelley made in thinking that the idea of beauty could become incarnate for him in any earthly

form : while the *Hymn to Intellectual Beauty* recognizes
the truth that such realization of the ideal is impossible.
The very last letter written by Shelley sets the miscon-
ception in its proper light : " I think one is always in
love with something or other; the error, and I confess it
is not easy for spirits cased in flesh and blood to avoid it,
consists in seeking in a mortal image the likeness of what
is, perhaps, eternal." But this Shelley discovered only
with "the years that bring the philosophic mind," and
when he was upon the very verge of his untimely death.

The following quotation is a fair specimen of the blank
verse of *Alastor*. It expresses that longing for perfect
sympathy in an ideal love, which the sense of divine
beauty had stirred in the poet's heart :—

> At length upon the lone Chorasmian shore
> He paused, a wide and melancholy waste
> Of putrid marshes. A strong impulse urged
> His steps to the sea-shore. A swan was there,
> Beside a sluggish stream among the reeds.
> It rose as he approached, and, with strong wings
> Scaling the upward sky, bent its bright course
> High over the immeasurable main.
> His eyes pursued its flight :—" Thou hast a home,
> Beautiful bird ! thou voyagest to thine home,
> Where thy sweet mate will twine her downy neck
> With thine, and welcome thy return with eyes
> Bright in the lustre of their own fond joy.
> And what am I that I should linger here,
> With voice far sweeter than thy dying notes,
> Spirit more vast than thine, frame more attuned
> To beauty, wasting these surpassing powers
> In the deaf air, to the blind earth, and heaven
> That echoes not my thoughts ? " A gloomy smile
> Of desperate hope wrinkled his quivering lips.
> For Sleep, he knew, kept most relentlessly
> Its precious charge, and silent Death exposed,
> Faithless perhaps as Sleep, a shadowy lure,
> With doubtful smile mocking its own strange charms.

William, the eldest son of Shelley and Mary Godwin, was born on the 24th of Jan., 1816. In the spring of that year they went together, accompanied by Miss Clairmont, for a second time to Switzerland. They reached Geneva on the 17th of May, and were soon after joined by Lord Byron and his travelling physician, Dr. Polidori. Shelley had not yet made Byron's acquaintance, though he had sent him a copy of *Queen Mab*, with a letter, which miscarried in the post. They were now thrown into daily intercourse, occupying the villas Diodati and Mont Alégre at no great distance from each other, passing their days upon the lake in a boat which they purchased, and spending the nights in conversation. Miss Clairmont had known Byron in London, and their acquaintance now ripened into an intimacy, the fruit of which was the child Allegra. This fact has to be mentioned by Shelley's biographer, because Allegra afterwards became an inmate of his home ; and though he and Mary were ignorant of what was passing at Geneva, they did not withdraw their sympathy from the mother of Lord Byron's daughter. The lives of Byron and Shelley during the next six years were destined to be curiously blent. Both were to seek in Italy an exile-home ; while their friendship was to become one of the most interesting facts of English literary history. The influence of Byron upon Shelley, as he more than once acknowledged, and as his wife plainly perceived, was, to a great extent, depressing. For Byron's genius and its fruits in poetry he entertained the highest possible opinion. He could not help comparing his own achievement and his fame with Byron's ; and the result was that in the presence of one whom he erroneously believed to be the greater poet, he became inactive. Shelley, on the contrary, stimulated

Byron's productive faculty to nobler efforts, raised his
moral tone, and infused into his less subtle intellect
something of his own philosophical depth and earnestness.   Much as he enjoyed Byron's society and admired
his writing, Shelley was not blind to the imperfections of
his nature.   The sketch which he has left us of Count
Maddalo, the letters written to his wife from Venice and
Ravenna, and his correspondence on the subject of Leigh
Hunt's visit to Italy, supply the most discriminating
criticism which has yet been passed upon his brother poet's
character.   It is clear that he never found in Byron a perfect friend, and that he had not accepted him as one with
whom he sympathized upon the deeper questions of feeling
and conduct.   Byron, for his part, recognized in Shelley
the purest nature he had ever known.   " He was the most
gentle, the most amiable, and least worldly-minded person
I ever met; full of delicacy, disinterested beyond all
other men, and possessing a degree of genius joined to
simplicity as rare as it is admirable.   He had formed to
himself a *beau ideal* of all that is fine, high-minded, and
noble, and he acted up to this ideal even to the very
letter."

Toward the end of June the two poets made the tour
of Lake Geneva in their boat, and were very nearly
wrecked off the rocks of Meillerie.   On this occasion
Shelley was in imminent danger of death from drowning.
His one anxiety, however, as he wrote to Peacock, was
lest Byron should attempt to save him at the risk of his
own life.   Byron described him as "bold as a lion ;" and
indeed it may here be said, once and for all, that Shelley's
physical courage was only equalled by his moral fearless-
ness.   He carried both without bravado to the verge of
temerity, and may justly be said to have never known

what terror was. Another summer excursion was a visit
to Chamouni, of which he has left memorable descriptions in his letters to Peacock, and in the somewhat
Coleridgian verses on Mont Blanc. The preface to *Laon
and Cythna* shows what a powerful impression had been
made upon him by the glaciers, and how he delighted in
the element of peril. There is a tone of exultation in the
words which record the experiences of his two journeys in
Switzerland and France :—" I have been familiar from
boyhood with mountains and lakes and the sea, and the
solitude of forests. Danger, which sports upon the brink
of precipices, has been my playmate. I have trodden
the glaciers of the Alps, and lived under the eye of Mont
Blanc. I have been a wanderer among distant fields.
I have sailed down mighty rivers, and seen the sun rise
and set, and the stars come forth, whilst I have sailed
night and day down a rapid stream among mountains. I
have seen populous cities, and have watched the passions
which rise and spread, and sink and change amongst
assembled multitudes of men. I have seen the theatre
of the more visible ravages of tyranny and war, cities
and villages reduced to scattered groups of black and
roofless houses, and the naked inhabitants sitting famished
upon their desolated thresholds."

On their return to the lake, the Shelleys found M. G.
Lewis established with Byron. This addition to the
circle introduced much conversation about apparitions,
and each member of the party undertook to produce a
ghost story. Polidori's *Vampyre* and Mrs. Shelley's
Frankenstein were the only durable results of their determination. But an incident occurred which is of some
importance in the history of Shelley's psychological condition. Toward midnight on the 18th of July, Byron

recited the lines in *Christabel* about the lady's breast;
when Shelley suddenly started up, shrieked, and fled
from the room.   He had seen a vision of a woman with
eyes instead of nipples.   At this time he was writing notes
upon the phenomena of sleep to be inserted in his *Speculations on Metaphysics*, and Mrs. Shelley informs us that
the mere effort to remember dreams of thrilling or mysterious import so disturbed his nervous system that he
had to relinquish the task.   At no period of his life was
he wholly free from visions which had the reality of
facts.   Sometimes they occurred in sleep and were pro-
longed with painful vividness into his waking moments.
Sometimes they seemed to grow out of his intense medi-
tation, or to present themselves before his eyes as the
projection of a powerful inner impression.   All his sensations were abnormally acute, and his ever-active imagination confused the border-lands of the actual and the
visionary.   Such a nature as Shelley's, through its far
greater susceptibility than is common even with artistic
temperaments, was debarred in moments of high-strung
emotion from observing the ordinary distinctions of
subject and object; and this peculiar quality must never
be forgotten when we seek to estimate the proper proportions of *Dichtung und Wahrheit* in certain episodes of
his biography.   The strange story, for example, told by
Peacock about a supposed warning he had received in the
spring of this year from Mr. Williams of Tremadoc, may
possibly be explained on the hypothesis that his brooding
thoughts had taken form before him, both ear and eye
having been unconsciously pressed into the service of a
subjective energy.[1]

On their return to England in September, Shelley took

[1] Fraser's Magazine, Jan., 1860, p. 98.

a cottage at Great Marlow on the Thames, in order to be near his friend Peacock. While it was being prepared for the reception of his family, he stayed at Bath, and there heard of Harriet's suicide. The life that once was dearest to him, had ended thus in misery, desertion, want. The mother of his two children, abandoned by both her husband and her lover, and driven from her father's home, had drowned herself after a brief struggle with circumstance. However Shelley may have felt that his conscience was free from blame, however small an element of self-reproach may have mingled with his grief and horror, there is no doubt that he suffered most acutely. His deepest ground for remorse seems to have been the conviction that he had drawn Harriet into a sphere of thought and feeling for which she was not qualified, and that had it not been for him and his opinions, she might have lived a happy woman in some common walk of life. One of his biographers asserts that " he continued to be haunted by certain recollections, partly real and partly imaginative, which pursued him like an Orestes," and even Trelawny, who knew him only in the last months of his life, said that the impression of that dreadful moment was still vivid. We may trace the echo of his feelings in some painfully pathetic verses written in 1817 ; [1] and though he did not often speak of Harriet, Peacock has recorded one memorable occasion on which he disclosed the anguish of his spirit to a friend. [2]

Shelley hurried at once to London, and found some consolation in the society of Leigh Hunt. The friendship extended to him by that excellent man at this season of his trouble may perhaps count for something with

[1] Forman, iii. 148.
[2] Fraser, Jan., 1860, p. 102.

those who are inclined to judge him harshly. Two important events followed immediately upon the tragedy.
The first was Shelley's marriage with Mary Godwin on
the 30th of December, 1816. Whether Shelley would
have taken this step except under strong pressure from
without, appears to me very doubtful. Of all men who ever
lived, he was the most resolutely bent on confirming his
theories by his practice ; and in this instance there was no
valid reason why he should not act up to principles professed
in common by himself and the partner of his fortunes, no less
than by her father and her mother. It is, therefore, reason-
able to suppose that he yielded to arguments ; and these
arguments must have been urged by Godwin, who had never
treated him with cordiality since he left England in 1816.
Godwin, though overrated in his generation and almost
ludicrously idealized by Shelley, was a man whose talents
verged on genius. But he was by no means consistent.
His conduct in money-matters shows that he could not
live the life of a self-sufficing philosopher ; while the irritation he expressed when Shelley omitted to address him
as Esquire, stood in comic contradiction with his published
doctrines. We are therefore perhaps justified in concluding
that he worried Shelley, the one enthusiastic and thorough-
going follower he had, into marrying his daughter in spite
of his disciple's protestations ; nor shall we be far wrong
if we surmise that Godwin congratulated himself on Mary's
having won the right to bear the name of a future baronet.

The second event was the refusal of Mr. Westbrook
to deliver up the custody of his grandchildren. A
chancery suit was instituted ; at the conclusion of which,
in August, 1817, Lord Eldon deprived Shelley of his son
and daughter on the double ground of his opinions expressed in *Queen Mab*, and of his conduct toward his first

wife. The children were placed in the hands of a clergyman, to be educated in accordance with principles dia-
metrically opposed to their parent's, while Shelley's income
was mulcted in a sum of 200*l.* for their maintenance.
Thus sternly did the father learn the value of that ancient
Æschylean maxim, τῷ δράσαντι παθεῖν, the doer of the deed
must suffer. His own impulsiveness, his reckless assump-
tion of the heaviest responsibilities, his overweening
confidence in his own strength to move the weight of the
world's opinions, had brought him to this tragic pass—to
the suicide of the woman who had loved him, and to the
sequestration of the offspring whom he loved.

Shelley is too great to serve as text for any sermon; and
yet we may learn from him as from a hero of Hebrew or
Hellenic story. His life was a tragedy ; and like some pro-
tagonist of Greek drama, he was capable of erring and of
suffering greatly. He had kicked against the altar of justice
as established in the daily sanctities of human life ; and
now he had to bear the penalty. The conventions he despised and treated like the dust beneath his feet, were found
in this most cruel crisis to be a rock on which his very
heart was broken. From this rude trial of his moral nature
he arose a stronger being ; and if longer life had been
granted him, he would undoubtedly have presented the en-
nobling spectacle of one who had been lessoned by his
own audacity, and by its bitter fruits, into harmony with
the immutable laws which he was ever seeking to obey.
It is just this conflict between the innate rectitude of
Shelley's over-daring nature and the circumstances of
ordinary existence, which makes his history so tragic :
and we may justly wonder whether, when he read the
Sophoclean tragedies of Œdipus, he did not apply their
doctrine of self-will and Nemesis to his own fortunes.

CHAPTER V.

AMID the torturing distractions of the Chancery suit about his children, and the still more poignant anguish of his own heart, and with the cloud of what he thought swift-coming death above his head, Shelley worked steadily, during the summer of 1817, upon his poem of *Laon and Cythna*. Six months were spent in this task. "The poem," to borrow Mrs. Shelley's words, "was written in his boat, as it floated under the beech-groves of Bisham, or during wanderings in the neighbouring country, which is distinguished for peculiar beauty." Whenever Shelley could, he composed in the open air. The terraces of the Villa Cappuccini at Este, and the Baths of Caracalla were the birthplace of *Prometheus*. *The Cenci* was written on the roof of the Villa Valsovano at Leghorn. The Cascine of Florence, the pine-woods near Pisa, the lawns above San Giuliano, and the summits of the Euganean Hills, witnessed the creation of his loveliest lyrics; and his last great poem, the *Triumph of Life*, was transferred to paper in his boat upon the Bay of Spezia.

If *Alastor* had expressed one side of Shelley's nature, his devotion to Ideal Beauty, *Laon and Cythna* was in a far profounder sense representative of its author. All his previous experiences and all his aspirations—his pas-

sionate belief in friendship, his principle of the equality of
women with men, his demand for bloodless revolution, his
confidence in eloquence and reason to move nations, his
doctrine of free love, his vegetarianism, his hatred of
religious intolerance and tyranny—are blent together and
concentrated in the glowing cantos of this wonderful
romance. The hero, Laon, is himself idealized, the self
which he imagined when he undertook his Irish campaign.
The heroine, Cythna, is the helpmate he had always
dreamed, the woman exquisitely feminine, yet capable of
being fired with male enthusiasms, and of grappling the
real problems of our nature with a man's firm grasp. In
the first edition of the poem he made Laon and Cythna
brother and sister, not because he believed in the desirability of incest, but because he wished to throw a glove
down to society, and to attack the intolerance of custom
in its stronghold. In the preface, he tells us that it was
his purpose to kindle in the bosoms of his readers "a
virtuous enthusiasm for those doctrines of liberty and
justice, that faith and hope in something good, which
neither violence, nor misrepresentation, nor prejudice, can
ever wholly extinguish among mankind;" to illustrate
"the growth and progress of individual mind aspiring
after excellence, and devoted to the love of mankind;"
and to celebrate Love "as the sole law which should
govern the moral world." The wild romantic treatment
of this didactic motive makes the poem highly
characteristic of its author. It is written in Spenserian
stanzas, with a rapidity of movement and a dazzling
brilliance that are Shelley's own. The story relates the
kindling of a nation to freedom at the cry of a young
poet-prophet, the temporary triumph of the good cause,
the final victory of despotic force, and the martyrdom

of the hero, together with whom the heroine falls a willing victim. It is full of thrilling incidents and lovely pictures; yet the tale is the least part of the poem; and few readers have probably been able either to sympathize with its visionary characters, or to follow the narrative without weariness. As in the case of other poems by Shelley—especially those in which he attempted to tell a story, for which kind of art his genius was not well suited—the central motive of *Laon and Cythna* is surrounded by so radiant a photosphere of imagery and eloquence that it is difficult to fix our gaze upon it, blinded as we are by the excess of splendour. Yet no one now can read the terrible tenth canto, or the lovely fifth, without feeling that a young eagle of poetry had here tried the full strength of his pinions in their flight. This truth was by no means recognized when *Laon and Cythna* first appeared before the public. Hooted down, derided, stigmatized, and howled at, it only served to intensify the prejudice with which the author of *Queen Mab* had come to be regarded.

I have spoken of this poem under its first name of *Laon and Cythna*. A certain number of copies were issued with this title;[1] but the publisher, Ollier, not without reason dreaded the effect the book would make; he therefore induced Shelley to alter the relationship between the hero and his bride, and issued the old sheets with certain cancelled pages under the title of *Revolt of Islam*. It was published in January, 1818. While still resident at Marlow, Shelley began two autobiographical poems—the one *Prince*

---

[1] How many copies were put in circulation is not known. There must certainly have been many more than the traditional three; for when I was a boy at Harrow, I picked up two uncut copies in boards at a Bristol bookshop, for the price of 2s. 6d. a piece.

Athanase, which he abandoned as too introspective and morbidly self-analytical, the other *Rosalind and Helen*, which he finished afterwards in Italy. Of the second of these compositions he entertained a poor opinion; nor will it bear comparison with his best work. To his biographer its chief interest consists in the character of Lionel, drawn less perhaps exactly from himself than as an ideal of the man he would have wished to be. The poet in *Alastor*, Laon in the *Revolt of Islam*, Lionel in *Rosalind and Helen*, and Prince Athanase, are in fact a remarkable row of self-portraits, varying in the tone and scale of idealistic treatment bestowed upon them. Later on in life, Shelley outgrew this preoccupation with his idealized self, and directed his genius to more objective themes. Yet the autobiographic tendency, as befitted a poet of the highest lyric type, remained to the end a powerful characteristic.

Before quitting the first period of Shelley's development, it may be well to set before the reader a specimen of that self-delineative poetry which characterized it; and since it is difficult to detach a single passage from the continuous stanzas of *Laon and Cythna*, I have chosen the lines in *Rosalind and Helen* which describe young Lionel:

> To Lionel,
> Though of great wealth and lineage high,
> Yet through those dungeon walls there came
> Thy thrilling light, O Liberty!
> And as the meteor's midnight flame
> Startles the dreamer, sun-like truth
> Flashed on his visionary youth,
> And filled him, not with love, but faith,
> And hope, and courage mute in death;
> For love and life in him were twins,
> Born at one birth: in every other
> First life, then love its course begins,

Though they be children of one mother;
And so through this dark world they fleet
Divided, till in death they meet:
But he loved all things ever.　Then
He past amid the strife of men,
And stood at the throne of arméd power
Pleading for a world of woe:
Secure as one on a rock-built tower
O'er the wrecks which the surge trails to and fro,
'Mid the passions wild of human kind
He stood, like a spirit calming them;
For, it was said, his words could find
Like music the lulled crowd, and stem
That torrent of unquiet dream,
Which mortals truth and reason deem,
But *is* revenge and fear and pride.
Joyous he was; and hope and peace
On all who heard him did abide,
Raining like dew from his sweet talk,
As where the evening star may walk
Along the brink of the gloomy seas,
Liquid mists of splendour quiver.
His very gestures touch'd to tears
The unpersuaded tyrant, never
So moved before: his presence stung
The torturers with their victim's pain,
And none knew how; and through their ears,
The subtle witchcraft of his tongue
Unlocked the hearts of those who keep
Gold, the world's bond of slavery.
Men wondered, and some sneer'd to see
One sow what he could never reap:
For he is rich, they said, and young,
And might drink from the depths of luxury.
If he seeks Fame, Fame never crown'd
The champion of a trampled creed:
If he seeks Power, Power is enthroned
'Mid ancient rights and wrongs, to feed
Which hungry wolves with praise and spoil,
Those who would sit near Power must toil;
And such, there sitting, all may see.

During the year he spent at Marlow, Shelley was a frequent visitor at Leigh Hunt's Hampstead house, where he made acquaintance with Keats, and the brothers Smith, authors of *Rejected Addresses*. Hunt's recollections supply some interesting details, which, since Hogg and Peacock fail us at this period, may be profitably used. Describing the manner of his life at Marlow, Hunt writes as follows : "He rose early in the morning, walked and read before breakfast, took that meal sparingly, wrote and studied the greater part of the morning, walked and read again, dined on vegetables (for he took neither meat nor wine), conversed with his friends (to whom his house was ever open), again walked out, and usually finished with reading to his wife till ten o'clock, when he went to bed. This was his daily existence. His book was generally Plato, or Homer, or one of the Greek tragedians, or the Bible, in which last he took a great, though peculiar, and often admiring interest. One of his favourite parts was the book of Job." Mrs. Shelley in her note on the *Revolt of Islam,* confirms this account of his Bible studies ; and indeed the influence of the Old Testament upon his style may be traced in several of his poems. In the same paragraph from which I have just quoted, Leigh Hunt gives a just notion of his relation to Christianity, pointing out that he drew a distinction between the Pauline presentation of the Christian creeds, and the spirit of the Gospels. "His want of faith in the letter, and his exceeding faith in the spirit of Christianity, formed a comment, the one on the other, very formidable to those who chose to forget what Scripture itself observes on that point." We have only to read Shelley's *Essay on Christianity,* in order to perceive what reverent admiration he felt for Jesus, and how profoundly he understood the true character of his teaching.

That work, brief as it is, forms one of the most valuable
extant contributions to a sound theology, and is morally far
in advance of the opinions expressed by many who regard
themselves as specially qualified to speak on the subject.
It is certain that, as Christianity passes beyond its
mediæval phase, and casts aside the husk of out-worn
dogmas, it will more and more approximate to Shelley's
exposition.　Here and here only is a vital faith, adapted
to the conditions of modern thought, indestructible
because essential, and fitted to unite instead of separating
minds of divers quality.　It may sound paradoxical to
claim for Shelley of all men a clear insight into the
enduring element of the Christian creed ; but it was
precisely his detachment from all its accidents which
enabled him to discern its spiritual purity, and placed
him in a true relation to its Founder.　For those who
would neither on the one hand relinquish what is permanent in religion, nor yet on the other deny the inevitable
conclusions of modern thought, his teaching is indubitably valuable.　His fierce tirades against historic
Christianity must be taken as directed against an
ecclesiastical system of spiritual tyranny, hypocrisy,
and superstition, which in his opinion had retarded the
growth of free institutions, and fettered the human
intellect.　Like Campanella, he distinguished between
Christ, who sealed the gospel of charity with his blood,
and those Christians, who would be the first to crucify
their Lord if he returned to earth.

That Shelley lived up to his religious creed is amply
proved.　To help the needy and to relieve the sick,
seemed to him a simple duty, which he cheerfully discharged.　" His charity, though liberal, was not weak.
He inquired personally into the circumstances of his

petitioners, visited the sick in their beds, ... and kept a regular list of industrious poor, whom he assisted with small sums to make up their accounts." At Marlow, the miserable condition of the lace-makers called forth all his energies; and Mrs. Shelley tells us that an acute ophthalmia, from which he twice suffered, was contracted in a visit to their cottages. A story told by Leigh Hunt about his finding a woman ill on Hampstead Heath, and carrying her from door to door in the vain hopes of meeting with a man as charitable as himself, until he had to house the poor creature with his friends the Hunts, reads like a practical illustration of Christ's parable about the the Good Samaritan. Nor was it merely to the so-called poor that Shelley showed his generosity. His purse was always open to his friends. Peacock received from him an annual allowance of 100*l.* He gave Leigh Hunt, on one occasion, 1400*l.*; and he discharged debts of Godwin, amounting, it is said, to about 6000*l.* In his pamphlet on *Putting Reform to the Vote*, he offered to subscribe 100*l.* for the purpose of founding an association; and we have already seen that he headed the Tremadoc subscription with a sum of 500*l.* These instances of his generosity might be easily multiplied; and when we remember that his present income was 1000*l.*, out of which 200*l.* went to the support of his children, it will be understood not only that he could not live luxuriously, but also that he was in frequent money difficulties through the necessity of raising funds upon his expectations. His self-denial in all minor matters of expenditure was conspicuous. Without a murmur, without ostentation, this heir of the richest baronet in Sussex illustrated by his own conduct those principles of democratic simplicity and of fraternal charity which formed his political and social creed.

A glimpse into the cottage at Great Marlow is afforded by a careless sentence of Leigh Hunt's. " He used to sit in a study adorned with casts, as large as life, of the Vatican Apollo and the celestial Venus." Fancy Shelley with his bright eyes and elf-locks in a tiny, low-roofed room, correcting proofs of *Laon and Cythna*, between the Apollo of the Belvedere and the Venus de' Medici, life-sized, and as crude as casts by Shout could make them! In this house, Miss Clairmont, with her brother and Allegra, lived as Shelley's guests; and here Clara Shelley was born on the 3rd of September, 1817. In the same autumn, Shelley suffered from a severe pulmonary attack. The critical state of his health and the apprehension, vouched for by Mrs. Shelley, that the Chancellor might lay his vulture's talons on the children of his second marriage, were the motives which induced him to leave England for Italy in the spring of 1818.[1] He never returned. Four years only of life were left to him—years filled with music that will sound as long as English lasts.

It was on the 11th of March that the Shelleys took their departure with Miss Clairmont and the child Allegra. They went straight to Milan, and after visiting the Lake of Como, Pisa, the Bagni di Lucca, Venice, and Rome, they settled early in the following December at Naples. Shelley's letters to Peacock form the invaluable record of this period of his existence. Taken altogether, they are the most perfect specimens of descriptive prose in the English language; never over-charged with colour, vibrating with emotions excited by the stimulating scenes of Italy, frank in criticism, and exquisitely delicate in observation. Their transparent sincerity and unpre-

[1] See Note on Poems of 1819, and compare the lyric " The billows on the beach."

meditated grace, combined with natural finish of expression, make them masterpieces of a style at once familiar
and elevated.   That Shelley's sensibility to art was not so
highly cultivated as his feeling for nature, is clear enough
in many passages : but there is no trace of admiring
to order in his comments upon pictures or statues.
Familiarity with the great works of antique and Italian
art would doubtless have altered some of the opinions
he at first expressed ; just as longer residence among
the people made him modify his views about their
character.   Meanwhile, the spirit of modest and unprejudiced attention in which he began his studies of
sculpture and painting, might well be imitated in the
present day by travellers who think that to pin their
faith to some famous critic's verdict is the acme of
good taste.   If there were space for a long quotation from
these letters, I should choose the description of Pompeii
(Jan. 26, 1819), or that of the Baths of Caracalla (March
23, 1819).   As it is, I must content myself with a short
but eminently characteristic passage, written from Ferrara,
Nov. 7, 1818 :—

> The handwriting of Ariosto is a small, firm, and pointed cha-
> racter, expressing, as I should say, a strong and keen, but
> circumscribed energy of mind ; that of Tasso is large, free, and
> flowing, except that there is a checked expression in the midst
> of its flow, which brings the letters into a smaller compass than
> one expected from the beginning of the word.   It is the symbol
> of an intense and earnest mind, exceeding at times its own depth,
> and admonished to return by the chillness of the waters of
> oblivion striking upon its adventurous feet.   You know I always
> seek in what I see the manifestation of something beyond the
> present and tangible object ; and as we do not agree in phy-
> siognomy, so we may not agree now.   But my business is to
> relate my own sensations, and not to attempt to inspire others
> with them.

In the middle of August, Shelley left his wife at the Bagni di Lucca, and paid a visit to Lord Byron at Venice. He arrived at midnight in a thunderstorm. *Julian and Maddalo* was the literary fruit of this excursion—a poem which has rightly been characterized by Mr. Rossetti as the most perfect specimen in our language of the "poetical treatment of ordinary things." The description of a Venetian sunset, touched to sadness amid all its splendour by the gloomy presence of the madhouse, ranks among Shelley's finest word-paintings; while the glimpse of Byron's life is interesting on a lower level. Here is the picture of the sunset and the island of San Lazzaro :—

> Oh!
> How beautiful is sunset, when the glow
> Of heaven descends upon a land like thee,
> Thou paradise of exiles, Italy,
> Thy mountains, seas, and vineyards, and the towers,
> Of cities they encircle !—It was ours
> To stand on thee, beholding it : and then,
> Just where we had dismounted, the Count's men
> Were waiting for us with the gondola.
> As those who pause on some delightful way,
> Though bent on pleasant pilgrimage, we stood
> Looking upon the evening, and the flood
> Which lay between the city and the shore,
> Paved with the image of the sky. The hoar
> And airy Alps, towards the north, appeared,
> Thro' mist, a heaven-sustaining bulwark, reared
> Between the east and west; and half the sky
> Was roofed with clouds of rich emblazonry,
> Dark purple at the zenith, which still grew
> Down the steep west into a wondrous hue
> Brighter than burning gold, even to the rent
> Where the swift sun yet paused in his descent
> Among the many-folded hills. They were
> Those famous Euganean hills, which bear,
> As seen from Lido through the harbour piles,

The likeness of a clump of peaked isles—
And then, as if the earth and sea had been
Dissolved into one lake of fire, were seen
Those mountains towering, as from waves of flame,
Around the vaporous sun, from which there came
The inmost purple spirit of light, and made
Their very peaks transparent. " Ere it fade,"
Said my companion, " I will show you soon
A better station." So, o'er the lagune
We glided ; and from that funereal bark
I leaned, and saw the city, and could mark
How from their many isles, in evening's gleam,
Its temples and its palaces did seem
Like fabrics of enchantment piled to heaven.
I was about to speak, when—" We are even
Now at the point I meant," said Maddalo,
And bade the gondolieri cease to row.
" Look, Julian, on the west, and listen well
If you hear not a deep and heavy bell."
I looked, and saw between us and the sun
A building on an island, such a one
As age to age might add, for uses vile,—
A windowless, deformed, and dreary pile ;
And on the top an open tower, where hung
A bell, which in the radiance swayed and swung,—
We could just hear its coarse and iron tongue :
The broad sun sank behind it, and it tolled
In strong and black relief—" What we behold
Shall be the madhouse and its belfry tower,"—
Said Maddalo ; " and ever at this hour,
Those who may cross the water hear that bell,
Which calls the maniacs, each one from his cell,
To vespers."

It may be parenthetically observed that one of the few
familiar quotations from Shelley's poems occurs in *Julian
and Maddalo :*—

                    Most wretched men
          Are cradled into poetry by wrong :
          They learn in suffering what they teach in song.

Byron lent the Shelleys his villa of the Cappuccini
near Este, where they spent some weeks in the autumn.
Here *Prometheus Unbound* was begun, and the *Lines
written among Euganean Hills* were composed; and here
Clara became so ill that her parents thought it necessary
to rush for medical assistance to Venice. They had
forgotten their passport; but Shelley's irresistible energy
overcame all difficulties, and they entered Venice—only in
time, however, for the child to die.

Nearly the whole of the winter was spent at Naples,
where Shelley suffered from depression of more than
ordinary depth. Mrs. Shelley attributed this gloom to
the state of his health; but Medwin tells a strange story,
which, if it is not wholly a romance, may better account
for the poet's melancholy. He says that so far back as
the year 1816, on the night before his departure from
London, " a married lady, young, handsome, and of noble
connexions," came to him, avowed the passionate love
she had conceived for him, and proposed that they should
fly together.[1] He explained to her that his hand and
heart had both been given irrevocably to another, and,
after the expression of the most exalted sentiments on
both sides, they parted. She followed him, however,
from place to place; and without intruding herself upon
his notice, found some consolation in remaining near
him. Now she arrived at Naples; and at Naples she died.
The web of Shelley's life was a wide one, and included more
destinies than his own. Godwin, as we have reason to
believe, attributed the suicide of Fanny Imlay to her
hopeless love for Shelley; and the tale of Harriet has been
already told. Therefore there is nothing absolutely

---

[1] Medwin's Life of Shelley, vol. i. 324. His date, 1814, appears
from the context to be a misprint.

improbable in Medwin's story, especially when we remember what Hogg half-humorously tells us about
Shelley's attraction for women in London. At any rate,
the excessive wretchedness of the lyrics written at Naples
can hardly be accounted for by the "constant and
poignant physical sufferings" of which Mrs. Shelley
speaks, since these were habitual to him. She was herself,
moreover, under the impression that he was concealing
something from her, and we know from her own words in
another place that his "fear to wound the feelings of
others" often impelled him to keep his deepest sorrows to
himself.[1]

All this while his health was steadily improving. The
menace of consumption was removed ; and though he
suffered from severe attacks of pain in the side, the cause
of this persistent malady does not seem to have been
ascertained. At Naples he was under treatment for
disease of the liver. Afterwards, his symptoms were
ascribed to nephritis ; and it is certain that his greater or
less freedom from uneasiness varied with the quality of
the water he drank. He was, for instance, forced to
eschew the drinking water of Ravenna, because it aggra-
vated his symptoms ; while Florence, for a similar reason,
proved an unsuitable residence. The final settlement of
the Shelleys at Pisa seems to have been determined by the
fact that the water of that place agreed with him. That
the spasms which from time to time attacked him were
extremely serious, is abundantly proved by the testimony
of those who lived with him at this period, and by his own
letters. Some relief was obtained by mesmerism, a remedy
suggested by Medwin ; but the obstinacy of the torment
preyed upon his spirits to such an extent, that even during

[1] Note on the Revolt of Islam.

the last months of his life we find him begging Trelawny to
procure him prussic acid as a final and effectual remedy for
all the ills that flesh is heir to. It may be added that
mental application increased the mischief, for he told Leigh
Hunt that the composition of *The Cenci* had cost him a
fresh seizure. Yet though his sufferings were indubitably
real, the eminent physician, Vaccà, could discover no
organic disease ; and possibly Trelawny came near the
truth when he attributed Shelley's spasms to insufficient
and irregular diet, and to a continual over-taxing of his
nervous system.

Mrs. Shelley states that the change from England to
Italy was in all respects beneficial to her husband. She
was inclined to refer the depression from which he
occasionally suffered, to his solitary habits ; and there are
several passages in his own letters which connect his
melancholy with solitude. It is obvious that when he
found himself in the congenial company of Trelawny,
Williams, Medwin, or the Gisbornes, he was simply happy ;
and nothing could be further from the truth than to paint
him as habitually sunk in gloom. On the contrary, we
hear quite as much about his high spirits, his " Homeric
laughter," his playfulness with children, his readiness to
join in the amusements of his chosen circle, and his
incomparable conversation, as we do about his solitary
broodings, and the seasons when pain or bitter memories
over-cast his heaven. Byron, who had some right to
express a judgment in such a matter, described him as the
most companionable man under the age of thirty he had
ever met with. Shelley rode and practised pistol-shooting
with his brother bard, sat up late to talk with him,
enjoyed his jokes, and even betted with him on one occasion marked by questionable taste. All this is quite

incompatible with that martyrdom to persecution, remorse,
or physical suffering, with which it has pleased some
romantic persons to invest the poet. Society of the
ordinary kind he hated. The voice of a stranger, or a
ring at the house-bell, heard from afar with Shelley's
almost inconceivable quickness of perception, was enough
to make him leave the house; and one of his prettiest
poems is written on his mistaking his wife's mention of
the Aziola, a little owl common enough in Tuscany, for an
allusion to a tiresome visitor. This dislike for intercourse
with commonplace people was the source of some disagree-
ment between him and Mrs. Shelley, and kept him
further apart from Byron than he might otherwise have
been. In a valuable letter recently published by Mr.
Garnett, he writes :—" I detest all society—almost all, at
least—and Lord Byron is the nucleus of all that is hateful
and tiresome in it." And again, speaking about his wife
to Trelawny, he said :—" She can't bear solitude, nor I
society—the quick coupled with the dead."

In the year 1818-19 the Shelleys had no friends at
all in Italy, except Lord Byron at Venice, and Mr. and
Mrs. John Gisborne at Leghorn. Mrs. Gisborne had been
a friend of Mary Wollstonecraft and Godwin. She was a
woman of much cultivation, devoid of prejudice, and,
though less enthusiastic than Shelley liked, quite capable of
appreciating the inestimable privilege of his acquaintance.
Her husband, to use a now almost obsolete phrase, was a
scholar and a gentleman. He shared his wife's enlightened
opinions, and remaind stanch through good and ill report to
his new friends. At Rome and Naples they knew absolutely
no one. Shelley's time was therefore passed in study and
composition. In the previous summer he had translated the
Symposium of Plato, and begun an essay on the Ethics

of the Greeks, which remains unluckily a fragment. Together with Mary he read much Italian literature, and his observations on the chief Italian poets form a valuable contribution to their criticism. While he admired the splendour and invention of Ariosto, he could not tolerate his moral tone. Tasso struck him as cold and artificial, in spite of his "delicate moral sensibility." Boccaccio he preferred to both; and his remarks on this prose-poet are extremely characteristic. "How much do I admire Boccaccio! What descriptions of nature are those in his little introductions to every new day! It is the morning of life stripped of that mist of familiarity which makes it obscure to us. Boccaccio seems to me to have possessed a deep sense of the fair ideal of human life, considered in its social relations. His more serious theories of love agree especially with mine. He often expresses things lightly too, which have serious meanings of a very beautiful kind. He is a moral casuist, the opposite of the Christian, stoical, ready-made, and worldly system of morals. Do you remember one little remark, or rather maxim of his, which might do some good to the common, narrow-minded conceptions of love,—'Bocca baciata non perde ventura; anzi rinnuova, come fa la luna'?" Dante and Petrarch remained the objects of his lasting admiration, though the cruel Christianity of the *Inferno* seemed to him an ineradicable blot upon the greatest of Italian poems. Of Petrarch's "tender and solemn enthusiasm," he speaks with the sympathy of one who understood the inner mysteries of idealizing love.

It will be gathered from the foregoing quotations that Shelley, notwithstanding his profound study of style and his exquisite perception of beauty in form and rhythm, required more than merely artistic ex-

cellences in poetry. He judged poems by their content
and spirit; and while he plainly expressed his abhorrence of the didactic manner, he held that art must be
moralized in order to be truly great.   The distinction he
drew between Theocritus and the earlier Greek singers
in the *Defence of Poetry,* his severe strictures on *The
Two Noble Kinsmen* in a letter to Mary (Aug. 20,
1818), and his phrase about Ariosto, "who is enter-
taining and graceful, and *sometimes* a poet," illustrate
the application of critical canons wholly at variance with
the "art for art" doctrine.

While studying Italian, he continued faithful to
Greek.   Plato was often in his hands, and the drama-
tists formed his almost inseparable companions.   How
deeply he felt the art of the Homeric poems, may
be gathered from the following extract :—"I congratu-
late you on your conquest of the Iliad.   You must have
been astonished at the perpetually increasing magnificence of the last seven books.   Homer there truly begins
to be himself.   The battle of the Scamander, the funeral
of Patroclus, and the high and solemn close of the whole
bloody tale in tenderness and inexpiable sorrow, are
wrought in a manner incomparable with anything of
the same kind.   The Odyssey is sweet, but there is nothing like this."   About this time, prompted by Mrs.
Gisborne, he began the study of Spanish, and conceived an
ardent admiration for Calderon, whose splendid and super-
natural fancy tallied with his own.   "I am bathing
myself in the light and odour of the starry Autos," he
writes to Mr. Gisborne in the autumn of 1820.   *Faust,*
too, was a favourite.   "I have been reading over and over
again *Faust,* and always with sensations which no other
composition excites.   It deepens the gloom and augments

the rapidity of ideas, and would therefore seem to me an
unfit study for any person who is a prey to the reproaches
of memory, and the delusions of an imagination not to be
restrained." The profound impression made upon him by
Margaret's story is expressed in two letters about Retzsch's
illustrations :—" The artist makes one envy his happiness
that he can sketch such things with calmness, which I
only dared look upon once, and which made my brain
swim round only to touch the leaf on the opposite side of
which I knew that it was figured."

The fruits of this occupation with Greek, Italian,
Spanish, and German were Shelley's translations from
Homer and Euripides, from Dante, from Calderon's *Magico
Prodigioso*, and from *Faust*, translations which have never
been surpassed for beauty of form and complete transfusion
of the spirit of one literature into the language of another.
On translation, however, he set but little store, asserting
that he only undertook it when he " could do absolutely
nothing else," and writing earnestly to dissuade Leigh
Hunt from devoting time which might be better spent, to
work of subordinate importance.[1] The following version
of a Greek epigram on Plato's spirit will illustrate his own
method of translation :—

> Eagle! why soarest thou above that tomb?
> To what sublime and star-y-paven home
>   Floatest thou?
> I am the image of swift Plato's spirit,
> Ascending heaven :—Athens does inherit
>   His corpse below.

Some time in the year 1820-21, he composed the *Defence of Poetry*, stimulated to this undertaking by his
friend Peacock's article on poetry, published in the

---

[1] Letter from Florence, Nov., 1819.

I

Literary Miscellany.[1] This essay not only sets forth his
theory of his own art, but it also contains some of his
finest prose writing, of which the following passage,
valuable alike for matter and style, may be cited as a
specimen :—

The functions of the poetical faculty are two-fold ; by one it
creates new materials of knowledge, and power, and pleasure ;
by the other it engenders in the mind a desire to reproduce and
arrange them according to a certain rhythm and order which
may be called the beautiful and the good.   The cultivation of
poetry is never more to be desired than at periods when, from an
excess of the selfish and calculating principle, the accumulation
of the materials of external life exceed the quantity of the
power of assimilating them to the internal laws of human nature.
The body has then become too unwieldy for that which
animates it.
Poetry is indeed something divine.   It is at once the centre
and circumference of knowledge ; it is that which comprehends
all science, and that to which all science must be referred.   It
is at the same time the root and blossom of all other systems
of thought ; it is that from which all spring, and that which
adorns all ; and that which, if blighted, denies the fruit and the
seed, and withholds from the barren world the nourishment and
the succession of the scions of the tree of life.   It is the perfect
and consummate surface and bloom of all things ; it is as the
odour and the colour of the rose to the texture of the elements
which compose it, as the form and splendour of unfaded beauty
to the secrets of anatomy and corruption.   What were virtue,
love, patriotism, friendship—what were the scenery of this beautiful universe which we inhabit ; what were our consolations on
this side of the grave—and what were our aspirations beyond it,
if poetry did not ascend to bring light and fire from those eternal
regions where the owl-winged faculty of calculation dare not ever
soar ?   Poetry is not like reasoning, a power to be exerted according to the determination of the will.   A man cannot say, "I will
compose poetry."   The greatest poet even cannot say it ; for the

---

[1] See Letter to Ollier, Jan. 20, 1820, Shelley Memorials, p.
135.

mind in creation is as a fading coal, which some invisible influence, like an inconstant wind, awakens to transitory brightness; this power arises from within, like the colour of a flower
which fades and changes as it is developed, and the conscious
portions of our natures are unprophetic either of its approach or
its departure. Could this influence be durable in its original
purity and force, it is impossible to predict the greatness of the
results; but when composition begins, inspiration is already on
the decline, and the most glorious poetry that has ever been
communicated to the world is probably a feeble shadow of the
original conceptions of the poet. I appeal to the greatest poets
of the present day, whether it is not an error to assert that the
finest passages of poetry are produced by labour and study. The
toil and the delay recommended by critics, can be justly inter-
preted to mean no more than a careful observation of the inspired moments, and an artificial connexion of the spaces
between their suggestions by the intertexture of conventional
expressions; a necessity only imposed by the limitedness of the
poetical faculty itself; for Milton conceived the "Paradise Lost"
as a whole before he executed it in portions. We have his own
authority also for the muse having "dictated" to him the "un-
premeditated song." And let this be an answer to those who
would allege the fifty-six various readings of the first line of the
"Orlando Furioso." Compositions so produced are to poetry
what mosaic is to painting. This instinct and intuition of the
poetical faculty is still more observable in the plastic and pic-
torial arts; a great statue or picture grows under the power
of the artist as a child in the mother's womb; and the very
mind which directs the hands in formation is incapable of
accounting to itself for the origin, the gradations, or the media
of the process.

Poetry is the record of the best and happiest moments of the
happiest and best minds. We are aware of evanescent visitations
of thought and feeling sometimes associated with place or person,
sometimes regarding our own mind alone, and always arising
unforeseen and departing unbidden, but elevating and delightful
beyond all expression: so that even in the desire and the regret
they leave, there cannot but be pleasure, participating as it does
in the nature of its object. It is as it were the interpenetration
of a diviner nature through our own; but its footsteps are like
those of a wind over the sea, which the coming calm erases, and

whose traces remain only, as on the wrinkled sand which paves it. These and corresponding conditions of being are experienced principally by those of the most delicate sensibility and the most enlarged imagination; and the state of mind produced by them is at war with every base desire. The enthusiasm of virtue, love, patriotism, and friendship, is essentially linked with such emotions; and whilst they last, self appears as what it is, an atom to a universe. Poets are not only subject to these experiences as spirits of the most refined organization, but they can colour all that they combine with the evanescent hues of this ethereal world; a word, a trait in the representation of a scene or a passion, will touch the enchanted chord, and reanimate, in those who have ever experienced these emotions, the sleeping, the cold, the buried image of the past. Poetry thus makes immortal all that is best and most beautiful in the world; it arrests the vanishing apparitions which haunt the interlunations of life, and veiling them, or in language or in form, sends them forth among mankind, bearing sweet news of kindred joy to those with whom their sisters abide—abide, because there is no portal of expression from the caverns of the spirit which they inhabit into the universe of things. Poetry redeems from decay the visitations of the divinity in man.

In the midst of these æsthetic studies, and while producing his own greatest works, Shelley was not satisfied that his genius ought to be devoted to poetry. "I consider poetry," he wrote to Peacock, January 26th, 1819, "very subordinate to moral and political science, and if I were well, certainly I would aspire to the latter; for I can conceive a great work, embodying the discoveries of all ages, and harmonizing the contending creeds by which mankind have been ruled. Far from me is such an attempt, and I shall be content, by exercising my fancy, to amuse myself, and perhaps some others, and cast what weight I can into the scale of that balance which the Giant of Arthegall holds." Whether he was right in the conviction that his genius was no less fitted for metaphysical speculation or for political

science than for poetry, is a question that admits of much
debate.[1] We have nothing but fragments whereby to
form a definite opinion—the unfinished *Defence of Poetry*,
the unfinished *Essay on a Future State*, the unfinished
Essay on Christianity, the unfinished *Essay on the Punishment of Death*, and the scattered *Speculations on Metaphysics*. None of these compositions justify the belief so
confidently expressed by Mrs. Shelley in her Preface to
the prose works, that "had not Shelley deserted metaphysics for poetry in his youth, and had he not been lost
to us early, so that all his vaster projects were wrecked
with him in the waves, he would have presented the
world with a complete theory of mind ; a theory to which
Berkeley, Coleridge, and Kant would have contributed ;
but more simple, unimpugnable, and entire than the systems
of these writers." Their incompleteness rather tends to
confirm what she proceeds to state, that the strain of
philosophical composition was too great for his susceptible nerves ; while her further observation that " thought
kindled imagination and awoke sensation, and rendered him dizzy from too great keenness of emotion,"
seems to indicate that his nature was primarily that
of a poet deeply tinctured with philosophical speculation, rather than that of a metaphysician warmed at
intervals to an imaginative fervour. Another of her
remarks confirms us in this opinion. " He considered
these philosophical views of mind and nature to be instinct with the intensest spirit of poetry."[2] This is the
position of the poet rather than the analyst ; and, on the
whole, we are probably justified in concluding with Mrs.

[1] See Mrs. Shelley's note on the Revolt of Islam, and the whole
Preface to the Prose Works.
[2] Note on Prometheus.

Shelley, that he followed a true instinct when he dedicated himself to poetry and trained his powers in that direction.[1] To dogmatize upon the topic would be worse than foolish. There was something incalculable, incommensurable, and dæmonic in Shelley's genius; and what he might have achieved, had his life been spared and had his health progressively improved, it is of course impossible to say.

In the spring of 1819 the Shelleys settled in Rome, where the poet proceeded with the composition of *Prometheus Unbound.* He used to write among the ruins of the Baths of Caracalla, not then, as now, despoiled of all their natural beauty, but waving with the Paradise of flowers and shrubs described in his incomparable letter of March the 23rd to Peacock. Rome, however, was not destined to retain them long. On the 7th of June they lost their son William after a short illness. Shelley loved this child intensely, and sat by his bedside for sixty hours without taking rest. He was now practically childless; and his grief found expression in many of his poems, especially in the fragment headed " *Roma, Roma, Roma ! non è più com' era prima.*" William was buried in the Protestant cemetery, of which Shelley had written a description to Peacock in the previous December. "The English burying-place is a green slope near the walls, under the pyramidal tomb of Cestius, and is, I think, the most beautiful and solemn cemetery I ever beheld. To see the sun shining on its bright grass, fresh, when we first visited it, with the autumnal dews, and hear the whispering of the wind among the leaves of the trees which have overgrown the tomb of Cestius, and the soil which is stirring in the sun-warm earth, and to mark the tombs,

---

[1] Note on Revolt of Islam.

mostly of women and young people who were buried
there, one might, if one were to die, desire the sleep they
seem to sleep.   Such is the human mind, and so it peoples
with its wishes vacancy and oblivion."

Escaping from the scene of so much sorrow, they
established themselves at the Villa Valsovano, near
Leghorn.   Here Shelley began and finished *The Cenci*
at the instance of his wife, who rightly thought that he
undervalued his own powers as a dramatic poet.   The
supposed portrait of Beatrice in the Barberini Palace had
powerfully affected his imagination, and he fancied that
her story would form the fitting subject for a tragedy.
It is fortunate for English literature that the real facts of
that domestic drama, as recently published by Signor
Bertolotti, were then involved in a tissue of romance and
legend.   During this summer he saw a great deal of the
Gisborne family.   Mrs. Gisborne's son by a previous
marriage, Henry Reveley, was an engineer, and Shelley
conceived a project of helping him to build a steamer
which should ply between Leghorn and Marseilles.   He
was to supply the funds, and the pecuniary profit was to
be shared by the Gisborne family.   The scheme eventually fell through, though Shelley spent a good deal of
money upon it ; and its only importance is the additional
light it throws upon his public and private benevolence.
From Leghorn the Shelleys removed in the autumn to
Florence, where, on the 12th of November, the present
Sir Percy Florence Shelley was born.   Here Shelley
wrote the last act of *Prometheus Unbound*, which, though
the finest portion of that unique drama, seems to
have been an afterthought.   In the Cascine outside
Florence he also composed the *Ode to the West Wind*,
the most symmetrically perfect as well as the most im-

passioned of his minor lyrics. He spent much time in
the galleries, made notes upon the principal antique
statues, and formed a plan of systematic art-study. The
climate, however, disagreed with him, and in the month
of January, 1820, they took up their abode at Pisa.

1819 was the most important year in Shelley's life, so
far as literary production is concerned. Besides *The Cenci*
and *Prometheus Unbound,* of which it yet remains to
speak, this year saw the production of several political
and satirical poems—the *Masque of Anarchy,* suggested by
the news of the Peterloo massacre, being by far the most
important. Shelley attempted the composition of short popular songs which should stir the English people to a sense
of what he felt to be their degradation. But he lacked the
directness which alone could make such verses forcible,
and the passionate apostrophe to the Men of England in
his *Masque of Anarchy* marks the highest point of his
achievement in this style :—

> Men of England, Heirs of Glory,
> Heroes of unwritten story,
> Nurslings of one mighty mother,
> Hopes of her, and one another !
>
> Rise, like lions after slumber,
> In unvanquishable number,
> Shake your chains to earth like dew,
> Which in sleep had fall'n on you.
> Ye are many, they are few.

Peter Bell the Third, written in this year, and *Swell-
foot the Tyrant,* composed in the following autumn,
are remarkable as showing with what keen interest
Shelley watched public affairs in England from his
exile home ; but for my own part, I cannot agree with

those critics who esteem their humour at a high rate.
The political poems may profitably be compared with his
contemporary correspondence ; with the letters, for instance, to Leigh Hunt, November 23rd, 1819 ; and to
Mr. John Gisborne, April 10th, 1822 ; and with an
undated fragment published by Mr. Garnett in the *Relics
of Shelley*, page 84. No student of English political
history before the Reform Bill can regard his apprehensions of a great catastrophe as ill-founded. His insight
into the real danger to the nation was as penetrating as
his suggestion of a remedy was moderate. Those who are
accustomed to think of the poet as a visionary enthusiast,
will rub their eyes when they read the sober lines in which
he warns his friend to be cautious about the security
offered by the English Funds. Another letter, dated
Lerici, June 29, 1822, illustrates the same practical temper
of mind, the same logical application of political principles
to questions of public economy.

That *Prometheus Unbound* and *The Cenci* should have
been composed in one and the same year must be reckoned
among the greatest wonders of literature, not only because
of their sublime greatness, but also because of their essential difference. Æschylus, it is well-known, had written
a sequel to his *Prometheus Bound*, in which he showed
the final reconciliation between Zeus, the oppressor, and
Prometheus, the champion, of humanity. What that
reconciliation was, we do not know, because the play is
lost, and the fragments are too brief for supporting any
probable hypothesis. But Shelley repudiated the notion
of compromise. He could not conceive of the Titan "un-
saying his high language and quailing before his successful
and perfidious adversary." He, therefore, approached the
theme of liberation from a wholly different point of view.

Prometheus in his drama is the humane vindicator of love,
justice, and liberty, as opposed to Jove, the tyrannical
oppressor, and creator of all evil by his selfish rule.
Prometheus is the mind of man idealized, the spirit of
our race, as Shelley thought it made to be. Jove is the
incarnation of all that thwarts its free development. Thus
counterposed, the two chief actors represent the fundamental antitheses of good and evil, liberty and despotism,
love and hate. They give the form of personality to
Shelley's Ormuzd-Ahriman dualism already expressed in
the first canto of *Laon and Cythna ;* but instead of being
represented on the theatre of human life, the strife is
now removed into the region of abstractions, vivified by
mythopoetry. Prometheus resists Jove to the uttermost,
endures all torments, physical and moral, that the tyrant
plagues him with, secure in his own strength and calmly
expectant of an hour which shall hurl Jove from heaven,
and leave the spirit of good triumphant. That hour
arrives ; Jove disappears ; the burdens of the world and
men are suddenly removed ; a new age of peace and
freedom and illimitable energy begins ; the whole universe
partakes in the emancipation ; the spirit of the earth no
longer groans in pain, but sings alternate love-songs with
his sister orb, the moon ; Prometheus is re-united in
indissoluble bonds to his old love, Asia. Asia, withdrawn
from sight during the first act, but spoken of as waiting
in her exile for the fated hour, is the true mate of the
human spirit. She is the fairest daughter of Earth and
Ocean. Like Aphrodite, she rises in the Ægean near the
land called by her name ; and in the time of tribulation she
dwells in a far Indian vale. She is the Idea of Beauty incarnate, the shadow of the Light of Life which sustains the
world and enkindles it with love, the reality of Alastor's

vision, the breathing image of the awful loveliness apostrophized in the *Hymn to Intellectual Beauty*, the reflex of the splendour of which Adonais was a part. At the moment of her triumph she grows so beautiful that Ione her sister cannot see her, only feels her influence. The essential thought of Shelley's creed was that the universe is penetrated, vitalized, made real by a spirit, which he sometimes called the Spirit of Nature, but which is always conceived as more than Life, as that which gives its actuality to Life, and lastly as Love and Beauty. To adore this spirit, to clasp it with affection, and to blend with it, is, he thought, the true object of man. Therefore, the final union of Prometheus with Asia is the consummation of human destinies. Love was the only law Shelley recognized. Unterrified by the grim realities of pain and crime revealed in nature and society, he held fast to the belief that, if we could but pierce to the core of things, if we could but be what we might be, the world and man would both attain to their perfection in eternal love. What resolution through some transcendental harmony was expected by Shelley for the palpable discords in the structure of the universe, we hardly know. He did not give his philosophy systematic form : and his new science of love remains a luminous poetic vision—nowhere more brilliantly set forth than in the "sevenfold hallelujahs and harping symphonies" of this, the final triumph of his lyrical poetry.

In *Prometheus*, Shelley conceived a colossal work of art, and sketched out the main figures on a scale of surpassing magnificence. While painting in these figures, he seems to reduce their proportions too much to the level of earthly life. He quits his god-creating, heaven-compelling throne of mythopœic inspiration, and descends to a love-story of Asia and Prometheus. In other words, he does not sustain the visionary and primeval dignity of these incarnated abstractions ; nor, on the other hand, has he so elaborated their characters in detail as to give them the substantiality of persons. There is therefore something vague and hollow in both figures. Yet in the subordinate passages of the poem, the true mythopœic faculty— the faculty of finding concrete forms for thought, and of investing emotion with personality—shines forth with extraordinary force and clearness. We feel ourselves in the grasp of a primitive myth-maker while we read the description of Oceanus, and the raptures of the Earth and Moon.

A genuine liking for *Prometheus Unbound* may be reckoned the touch-stone of a man's capacity for understanding lyric poetry. The world in which the action is supposed to move, rings with spirit voices ; and what these spirits sing, is melody more purged of mortal dross than any other poet's ear has caught, while listening to his own heart's song, or to the rhythms of the world. There are hymns in *Prometheus*, which seem to realize the miracle of making words, detached from meaning, the substance of a new ethereal music ; and yet although their verbal harmony is such, they are never devoid of definite significance for those who understand. Shelley scorned the æsthetics of a school which finds "sense swooning into nonsense" admirable. And if a critic is so dull as to ask what "Life of Life ! thy lips enkindle" means, or to whom it is addressed, none can help him any more than one can help a man whose sense of hearing is too gross for the tenuity of a bat's cry. A voice in the air thus sings the hymn of Asia at the moment of her apotheosis :—

Life of Life ! thy lips enkindle
　With their love the breath between them ;
And thy smiles before they dwindle
　Make the cold air fire ; then screen them
In those looks where whoso gazes
Faints, entangled in their mazes.

Child of Light ! thy limbs are burning
　Through the vest which seems to hide them,
As the radiant lines of morning
　Through the clouds, ere they divide them ;
And this atmosphere divinest
Shrouds thee wheresoe'er thou shinest.

Fair are others ; none beholds thee.
　But thy voice sounds low and tender,
Like the fairest, for it folds thee
　From the sight, that liquid splendour,
And all feel, yet see thee never,
As I feel now, lost for ever !

Lamp of Earth ! where'er thou movest
　Its dim shapes are clad with brightness,
And the souls of whom thou lovest
　Walk upon the winds with lightness,
Till they fail, as I am failing,
Dizzy, lost, yet unbewailing !

It has been said that Shelley, as a landscape painter, is
decidedly Turneresque ; and there is much in *Prometheus
Unbound* to justify this opinion. The scale of colour is
light and aerial, and the darker shadows are omitted. An
excess of luminousness seems to be continually radiated
from the objects at which he looks ; and in this radiation
of many-coloured lights, the outline itself is apt to be a
little misty. Shelley, moreover, pierced through things to
their spiritual essence. The actual world was less for him
than that which lies within it and beyond it. " I seek,"
he says himself, " in what I see, the manifestation of some-

thing beyond the present and tangible object." For him,
as for the poet described by one of the spirit voices in
Prometheus, the bees in the ivy-bloom are scarcely heeded;
they become in his mind,—

> Forms more real than living man,
> Nurslings of immortality.

And yet who could have brought the bees, the lake, the
sun, the bloom, more perfectly before us than that picture
does?[1] What vignette is more exquisitely coloured and
finished than the little study of a pair of halcyons in the
third act?[2] Blake is perhaps the only artist who could
have illustrated this drama. He might have shadowed
forth the choirs of spirits, the trailing voices and their
thrilling songs, phantasmal Demogorgon, and the charioted
Hour. Prometheus, too, with his "flowing limbs," has just
Blake's fault of impersonation—the touch of unreality in
that painter's Adam.

Passing to *The Cenci,* we change at once the moral and
artistic atmosphere. The lyrical element, except for one
most lovely dirge, is absent. Imagery and description
are alike sternly excluded. Instead of soaring to the
empyrean, our feet are firmly planted on the earth. In
exchange for radiant visions of future perfection, we are
brought into the sphere of dreadful passions—all the
agony, endurance, and half-maddened action, of which
luckless human innocence is capable. To tell the legend
of Beatrice Cenci here, is hardly needed. Her father, a
monster of vice and cruelty, was bent upon breaking her
spirit by imprisonment, torture, and nameless outrage. At
last her patience ended; and finding no redress in human
justice, no champion of her helplessness in living man, she

---

[1] Forman, vol. ii. p. 181.   [2] Ibid. p. 231.

wrought his death. For this she died upon the scaffold, together with her step-mother and her brothers, who had aided in the execution of the murder. The interest of *The Cenci,* and it is overwhelmingly great, centres in Beatrice and her father ; from these two chief actors in the drama, all the other characters fall away into greater or less degrees of unsubstantiality. Perhaps Shelley intended this—as the maker of a bas-relief contrives two or three planes of figures for the presentation of his ruling group. Yet there appears to my mind a defect of accomplishment, rather than a deliberate intention, in the delineation of Orsino. He seems meant to be the wily, crafty, Machiavellian reptile, whose calculating wickedness should form a contrast to the dæmonic, reckless, almost maniacal fiendishness of old Francesco Cenci. But this conception of him wavers ; his love for Beatrice is too delicately tinted, and he is suffered to break down with an infirmity of conscience alien to such a nature. On the other hand the uneasy vacillations of Giacomo, and the irresolution, born of feminine weakness and want of fibre, in Lucrezia, serve to throw the firm will of Beatrice into prominent relief ; while her innocence, sustained through extraordinary suffering in circumstances of exceptional horror—the innocence of a noble nature thrust by no act of its own but by its wrongs beyond the pale of ordinary womankind—is contrasted with the merely childish guiltlessness of Bernardo. Beatrice rises to her full height in the fifth act, dilates and grows with the approach of danger, and fills the whole scene with her spirit on the point of death. Her sublime confidence in the justice and essential rightness of her action, the glance of self-assured purity with which she annihilates the cut-throat brought to testify against her, her song in prison, and her

tender solicitude for the frailer Lucrezia, are used with
wonderful dramatic skill for the fulfilment of a feminine
ideal at once delicate and powerful. Once and once only
does she yield to ordinary weakness; it is when the
thought crosses her mind that she may meet her father in
the other world, as once he came to her on earth.

Shelley dedicated *The Cenci* to Leigh Hunt, saying that
he had striven in this tragedy to cast aside the subjective
manner of his earlier work, and to produce something at
once more popular and more concrete, more sober in style,
and with a firmer grasp on the realities of life. He was
very desirous of getting it acted, and wrote to Peacock
requesting him to offer it at Covent Garden. Miss O'Neil,
he thought, would play the part of Beatrice admirably. The
manager, however, did not take this view; averring that
the subject rendered it incapable of being even submitted
to an actress like Miss O'Neil. Shelley's self-criticism
is always so valuable, that it may be well here to collect
what he said about the two great dramas of 1819. Concerning *The Cenci* he wrote to Peacock :—" It is written
without any of the peculiar feelings and opinions which
characterise my other compositions; I having attended
simply to the impartial development of such characters, as
it is probable the persons represented really were,
together with the greatest degree of popular effect to be
produced by such a development." " *Cenci* is written
for the multitude, and ought to sell well." " I believe
it singularly fitted for the stage." " *The Cenci* is a
work of art; it is not coloured by my feelings, nor
obscured by my metaphysics. I don't think much of
it. It gave me less trouble than anything I have written
of the same length." *Prometheus*, on the other hand, he
tells Ollier, " is my favourite poem ; I charge you, there-

fore, specially to pet him and feed him with fine ink and good paper"—which was duly done. Again:—"For *Prometheus*, I expect and desire no great sale; *Prometheus* was never intended for more than five or six persons; it is in my judgment of a higher character than anything I have yet attempted, and is perhaps less an imitation of anything that has gone before it; it is original, and cost me severe mental labour." Shelley was right in judging that *The Cenci* would be comparatively popular; this was proved by the fact that it went through two editions in his lifetime. The value he set upon *Prometheus* as the higher work, will hardly be disputed. Unique in the history of literature, and displaying the specific qualities of its author at their height, the world could less easily afford to lose this drama than *The Cenci*, even though that be the greatest tragedy composed in English since the death of Shakespere. For reasons which will be appreciated by lovers of dramatic poetry, I refrain from detaching portions of these two plays. Those who desire to make themselves acquainted with their author's genius, must devote long and patient study to the originals in their entirety.

Prometheus Unbound, like the majority of Shelley's works, fell still-born from the press. It furnished punsters with a joke, however, which went the round of several papers; this poem, they cried, is well named, for who would bind it? Of criticism that deserves the name, Shelley got absolutely nothing in his lifetime. The stupid but venomous reviews which gove him occasional pain, but which he mostly laughed at, need not now be mentioned. It is not much to any purpose to abuse the authors of mere rubbish. The real lesson to be learned from such of them as may possibly have been sincere, as well as from the failure of his contemporaries to appreciate

K

his genius—the sneers of Moore, the stupidity of Campbell, the ignorance of Wordsworth, the priggishness of Southey, or the condescending tone of Keats —is that nothing is more difficult than for lesser men or equals to pay just homage to the greatest in their lifetime. Those who may be interested in studying Shelley's attitude toward his critics, should read a letter addressed to Ollier from Florence, October 15, 1819, soon after he had seen the vile attack upon him in the *Quarterly*, comparing this with the fragments of an expostulatory letter to the Editor, and the preface to *Adonais*.[1] It is clear that, though he bore scurrilous abuse with patience, he was prepared if needful to give blow for blow.   On the 11th of June, 1821, he wrote to Ollier:—"As yet I have laughed ; but woe to those scoundrels if they should once make me lose my temper !"   The stanzas on the *Quarterly* in *Adonais*, and the invective against Lord Eldon, show what Shelley could have done if he had chosen to castigate the curs.   Meanwhile the critics achieved what they intended.   Shelley, as Trelawny emphatically tells us, was universally shunned, coldly treated by Byron's friends at Pisa, and regarded as a monster by such of the English in Italy as had not made his personal acquaintance.   On one occasion he is even said to have been knocked down in a post-office by some big bully, who escaped before he could obtain his name and address ; but this is one of the stories rendered doubtful by lack of precise details.

[1] Shelley Memorials, p. 121.   Garnett's Relics of Shelley, pp. 49, 190.   Collected Letters, p. 147, in Moxon's Edition of Works in one vol. 1840.

CHAPTER VI.

RESIDENCE AT PISA.

ON the 26th of January, 1820, the Shelleys established
themselves at Pisa. From this date forward to the 7th of
July, 1822, Shelley's life divides itself into two periods of
unequal length ; the first spent at Pisa, the baths of San
Giuliano, and Leghorn ; the second at Lerici on the Bay
of Spezia. Without entering into minute particulars of
dates or recording minor changes of residence, it is possible to treat of the first and longer period in general.
The house he inhabited at Pisa was on the south side of
the Arno. After a few months he became the neighbour
of Lord Byron, who engaged the Palazzo Lanfranchi in
order to be near him ; and here many English and Italian
friends gathered round them. Among these must be
mentioned in the first place Captain Medwin, whose recollections of the Pisan residence are of considerable
value, and next Captain Trelawny, who has left a record
of Shelley's last days only equalled in vividness by
Hogg's account of the Oxford period, and marked by
signs of more unmistakable accuracy. Not less important members of this private circle were Mr. and Mrs.
Edward Elleker Williams, with whom Shelley and his
wife lived on terms of the closest friendship. Among

K 2

Italians, the physician Vaccà, the improvisatore Sgricci, and Rosini, the author of *La Monaca di Monza*, have to be recorded. It will be seen from this enumeration that Shelley was no longer solitary; and indeed it would appear that now, upon the eve of his accidental death, he had begun to enjoy an immunity from many of his previous sufferings. Life expanded before him: his letters show that he was concentrating his powers and preparing for a fresh flight; and the months, though ever productive of poetic masterpieces, promised a still more magnificent birth in the future.

In the summer and autumn of 1820, Shelley produced some of his most genial poems: the *Letter to Maria Gisborne*, which might be mentioned as a pendent to *Julian and Maddalo* for its treatment of familiar things; the *Ode to a Skylark*, that most popular of all his lyrics; the *Witch of Atlas*, unrivalled as an Ariel-flight of fairy fancy; and the *Ode to Naples*, which, together with the *Ode to Liberty*, added a new lyric form to English literature. In the winter he wrote the *Sensitive Plant*, prompted thereto, we are told, by the flowers which crowded Mrs. Shelley's drawing-room, and exhaled their sweetness to the temperate Italian sunlight. Whether we consider the number of these poems or their diverse character, ranging from verse separated by an exquisitely subtle line from simple prose to the most impassioned eloquence and the most ethereal imagination, we shall be equally astonished. Every chord of the poet's lyre is touched, from the deep bass string that echoes the diurnal speech of such a man as Shelley was, to the fine vibrations of a treble merging its rarity of tone in accents super-sensible to ordinary ears. One passage from the *Letter to Maria Gisborne* may here be

quoted, not for its poetry, but for the light it casts upon
the circle of his English friends.

> You are now
> In London, that great sea, whose ebb and flow
> At once is deaf and loud, and on the shore
> Vomits its wrecks, and still howls on for more.
> Yet in its depth what treasures ! You will see
> That which was Godwin,—greater none than he
> Though fallen—and fallen on evil times—to stand
> Among the spirits of our age and land,
> Before the dread tribunal of *To come*
> The foremost, while Rebuke cowers pale and dumb.
> You will see Coleridge—he who sits obscure
> In the exceeding lustre and the pure
> Intense irradiation of a mind,
> Which, with its own internal lightning blind,
> Flags wearily through darkness and despair—
> A cloud-encircled meteor of the air,
> A hooded eagle among blinking owls.
> You will see Hunt ; one of those happy souls
> Which are the salt of the earth, and without whom
> This world would smell like what it is—a tomb ;
> Who is, what others seem. His room no doubt
> Is still adorned by many a cast from Shout,
> With graceful flowers tastefully placed about ;
> And coronals of bay from ribbons hung,
> And brighter wreaths in neat disorder flung,
> The gifts of the most learn'd among some dozens
> Of female friends, sisters-in-law, and cousins.
> And there is he with his eternal puns,
> Which beat the dullest brain for smiles, like duns
> Thundering for money at a poet's door ;
> Alas ! it is no use to say, " I'm poor ! "—
> Or oft in graver mood, when he will look
> Things wiser than were ever read in book,
> Except in Shakespere's wisest tenderness.
> You will see Hogg ; and I cannot express
> His virtues, though I know that they are great,
> Because he locks, then barricades the gate

Within which they inhabit. Of his wit
And wisdom, you'll cry out when you are bit.
He is a pearl within an oyster-shell,
One of the richest of the deep. And there
Is English Peacock, with his mountain fair,—
Turn'd into a Flamingo, that shy bird
That gleams in the Indian air. Have you not heard
When a man marries, dies, or turns Hindoo,
His best friends hear no more of him. But you
Will see him, and will like him too, I hope,
With the milk-white Snowdonian antelope
Match'd with this camelopard. His fine wit
Makes such a wound, the knife is lost in it ;
A strain too learnèd for a shallow age,
Too wise for selfish bigots ; let his page
Which charms the chosen spirits of the time,
Fold itself up for the serener clime
Of years to come, and find its recompense
In that just expectation. Wit and sense,
Virtue and human knowledge ; all that might
Make this dull world a business of delight,
Are all combined in Horace Smith. And these,
With some exceptions, which I need not tease
Your patience by descanting on, are all
You and I know in London.

Captain Medwin, who came late in the autumn of
1820, at his cousin's invitation, to stay with the Shelleys,
has recorded many interesting details of their Pisan life,
as well as valuable notes of Shelley's conversation. " It
was nearly seven years since we had parted, but I should
have immediately recognized him in a crowd. His figure
was emaciated, and somewhat bent, owing to near-sighted-
ness, and his being forced to lean over his books, with
his eyes almost touching them ; his hair, still profuse,
and curling naturally, was partially interspersed with
grey ; but his appearance was youthful. There was also
a freshness and purity in his complexion that he never

lost." Not long after his arrival, Medwin suffered from a
severe and tedious illness. " Shelley tended me like a
brother. He applied my leeches, administered my medi-
cines, and during six weeks that I was confined to my
room, was assiduous and unintermitting in his affectionate
care of me." The poet's solitude and melancholy at this
time impressed his cousin very painfully. Though he
was producing a long series of imperishable poems, he did
not take much interest in his work. "I am disgusted
with writing," he once said, "and were it not for an
irresistible impulse, that predominates my better reason,
should discontinue so doing." The brutal treatment he
had lately received from the *Quarterly Review*, the
calumnies which pursued him, and the coldness of all but
a very few friends, checked his enthusiasm for composition. Of this there is abundant proof in his correspondence. In a letter to Leigh Hunt, dated Jan. 25,
1822, he says : "My faculties are shaken to atoms and
torpid. I can write nothing ; and if *Adonais* had no
success, and excited no interest, what incentive can I have
to write ?" Again: "I write little now. It is impossible to
compose except under the strong excitement of an assurance
of finding sympathy in what you write." Lord Byron's
company proved now, as before, a check rather than an
incentive to production: "I do not write ; I have lived
too long near Lord Byron, and the sun has extinguished
the glow-worm ; for I cannot hope, with St. John, that
the light came into the world and the world knew it not."
" I despair of rivalling Lord Byron, as well I may, and
there is no other with whom it is worth contending."
To Ollier, in 1820, he wrote : " I doubt whether I shall
write more. I could be content either with the hell or
the paradise of poetry ; but the torments of its purgatory

vex me, without exciting my powers sufficiently to put an
end to the vexation." It was not that his spirit was
cowed by the Reviews, or that he mistook the sort of
audience he had to address. He more than once acknowledged that, while Byron wrote for the many, his
poems were intended for the understanding few. Yet
the συνετοί, as he called them, gave him but scanty encouragement. The cold phrases of kindly Horace Smith
show that he had not comprehended *Prometheus Unbound ;*
and Shelley whimsically complains that even intelligent
and sympathetic critics confounded the ideal passion described in *Epipsychidion* with the love affairs of " a
servant-girl and her sweetheart." This almost incomprehensible obtuseness on the part of men who ought to
have known better, combined with the coarse abuse of
vulgar scribblers, was enough to make a man so sincerely
modest as Shelley doubt his powers, or shrink from the
severe labour of developing them.[1] " The decision of the
cause," he wrote to Mr. Gisborne, " whether or no *I* am a
poet, is removed from the present time to the hour when
our posterity shall assemble ; but the court is a very
severe one, and I fear that the verdict will be, guilty—
death." Deep down in his own heart he had, however,
less doubt : "This I know," he said to Medwin, " that
whether in prosing or in versing, there is something in
my writings that shall live for ever." And again he
writes to Hunt : "I am full of thoughts and plans, and
should do something, if the feeble and irritable frame
which encloses it was willing to obey the spirit. I fancy
that then I should do great things." It seems almost
certain that the incompleteness of many longer works

[1] See Medwin, vol. ii. p. 172, for Shelley's comment on the
difficulty of the poet's art.

designed in the Italian period, the abandonment of the tragedy on Tasso's story, the unfinished state of *Charles I.*, and the failure to execute the cherished plan of a drama suggested by the Book of Job, were due to the depressing effects of ill-health and external discouragement. Poetry with Shelley was no light matter. He composed under the pressure of intense excitement, and he elaborated his first draughts with minute care and severe self-criticism.

These words must not be taken as implying that he followed the Virgilian precedent of polishing and reducing the volume of his verses by an anxious exercise of calm reflection, or that he observed the Horatian maxim of deferring their publication till the ninth year. The contrary was notoriously the case with him. Yet it is none the less proved by the state of his manuscripts that his compositions, even as we now possess them, were no mere improvisations. The passage already quoted from his *Defence of Poetry* shows the high ideal he had conceived of the poet's duty toward his art; and it may be confidently asserted that his whole literary career was one long struggle to emerge from the incoherence of his earlier efforts, into the clearness of expression and precision of form that are the index of mastery over style. At the same time it was inconsistent with his most firmly rooted æsthetic principles, to attempt composition except under an impulse approaching to inspiration. To imperil his life by the fiery taxing of all his faculties, moral, intellectual and physical, and to undergo the discipline exacted by his own fastidious taste, with no other object in view than the frigid compliments of a few friends, was more than even Shelley's enthusiasm could endure. He, therefore, at this period required the powerful stimulus of some highly exciting cause from without to determine his activity.

Such external stimulus came to Shelley from three
quarters early in the year 1821. Among his Italian
acquaintances at Pisa, was a clever but disreputable Professor, of whom Medwin draws a very piquant portrait.
This man one day related the sad story of a beautiful and
noble lady, the Contessina Emilia Viviani, who had been
confined by her father in a dismal convent of the suburbs,
to await her marriage with a distasteful husband. Shelley,
fired as ever by a tale of tyranny, was eager to visit the
fair captive. The Professor accompanied him and Medwin
to the convent-parlour, where they found her more lovely
than even the most glowing descriptions had led them to
expect. Nor was she only beautiful. Shelley soon discovered that she had " cultivated her mind beyond what
I have ever met with in Italian women ;" and a rhapsody
composed by her upon the subject of Uranian Love—Il
Vero Amore—justifies the belief that she possessed an
intellect of more than ordinary elevation. He took Mrs.
Shelley to see her, and both did all they could to make her
convent-prison less irksome, by frequent visits, by letters,
and by presents of flowers and books. It was not long before
Shelley's sympathy for this unfortunate lady took the
form of love, which, however spiritual and Platonic, was
not the less passionate. The result was the composition of
Epipsychidion, the most unintelligible of all his poems
to those who have not assimilated the spirit of Plato's
Symposium and Dante's *Vita Nuova*. In it he apostro-
phizes Emilia Viviani as the incarnation of ideal beauty,
the universal loveliness made visible in mortal flesh :—

> Seraph of Heaven ! too gentle to be human,
> Veiling beneath that radiant form of woman
> All that is insupportable in thee
> Of light, and love, and immortality !

He tells her that he loves her, and describes the troubles
and deceptions of his earlier manhood, under allegories
veiled in deliberate obscurity. The Pandemic and the
Uranian Aphrodite have striven for his soul; for though
in youth he dedicated himself to the service of ideal
beauty, and seemed to find it under many earthly shapes,
yet has he ever been deluded. At last Emily appears,
and in her he recognizes the truth of the vision veiled
from him so many years. She and Mary shall henceforth,
like sun and moon, rule the world of love within him.
Then he calls on her to fly. They three will escape and
live together, far away from men, in an Ægean island.
The description of this visionary isle, and of the life to be
led there by the fugitives from a dull and undiscerning
world, is the most beautiful that has been written this
century in the rhymed heroic metre.

> It is an isle under Ionian skies,
> Beautiful as a wreck of Paradise;
> And, for the harbours are not safe and good,
> This land would have remained a solitude
> But for some pastoral people native there,
> Who from the Elysian, clear, and golden air
> Draw the last spirit of the age of gold,
> Simple and spirited, innocent and bold.
> The blue Ægean girds this chosen home,
> With ever-changing sound and light and foam
> Kissing the sifted sands and caverns hoar;
> And all the winds wandering along the shore
> Undulate with the undulating tide.
> There are thick woods where sylvan forms abide;
> And many a fountain, rivulet, and pond,
> As clear as elemental diamond,
> Or serene morning air. And far beyond,
> The mossy tracks made by the goats and deer,
> (Which the rough shepherd treads but once a year,)
> Pierce into glades, caverns, and bowers, and halls
> Built round with ivy, which the waterfalls

Illumining, with sound that never fails
Accompany the noonday nightingales ;
And all the place is peopled with sweet airs.
The light clear element which the isle wears
Is heavy with the scent of lemon-flowers,
Which floats like mist laden with unseen showers,
And falls upon the eyelids like faint sleep ;
And from the moss violets and jonquils peep,
And dart their arrowy odour through the brain,
Till you might faint with that delicious pain.
And every motion, odour, beam, and tone,
With that deep music is in unison :
Which is a soul within a soul—they seem
Like echoes of an antenatal dream.
It is an isle 'twixt heaven, air, earth, and sea,
Cradled, and hung in clear tranquillity ;
Bright as that wandering Eden, Lucifer,
Washed by the soft blue oceans of young air.
It is a favoured place.   Famine or Blight,
Pestilence, War, and Earthquake, never light
Upon its mountain-peaks ; blind vultures, they
Sail onward far upon their fatal way.
The wingèd storms, chanting their thunder-psalm
To other lands, leave azure chasms of calm
Over this isle, or weep themselves in dew,
From which its fields and woods ever renew
Their green and golden immortality.
And from the sea there rise, and from the sky
There fall, clear exhalations, soft and bright,
Veil after veil, each hiding some delight,
Which sun or moon or zephyr draws aside,
Till the isle's beauty, like a naked bride
Glowing at once with love and loveliness,
Blushes and trembles at its own excess :
Yet, like a buried lamp, a soul no less
Burns in the heart of this delicious isle,
An atom of the Eternal, whose own smile
Unfolds itself, and may be felt not seen
O'er the grey rocks, blue waves, and forests green,
Filling their bare and void interstices.

Shelley did not publish *Epipsychidion* with his own name. He gave it to the world as the composition of a man who had " died at Florence, as he was preparing for a voyage to one of the Sporades," and he requested Ollier not to circulate it, except among a few intelligent readers. It may almost be said to have been never published, in such profound silence did it issue from the press. Very shortly after its appearance he described it to Leigh Hunt as " a portion of me already dead," and added this significant allusion to its subject matter :—" Some of us have in a prior existence been in love with an Antigone, and that makes us find no full content in any mortal tie."   In the letter of June 18, 1822, again he says :—" The *Epipsychidion* I cannot look at ; the person whom it celebrates was a cloud instead of a Juno ; and poor Ixion starts from the Centaur that was the offspring of his own embrace. If you are curious, however, to hear what I am and have been, it will tell you something thereof. It is an idealized history of my life and feelings. I think one is always in love with something or other ; the error, and I confess it is not easy for spirits cased in flesh and blood to avoid it, consists in seeking in a mortal image the likeness of what is, perhaps, eternal." This paragraph contains the essence of a just criticism.   Brilliant as the poem is, we cannot read it with unwavering belief either in the author's sincerity at the time he wrote it, or in the permanence of the emotion it describes.   The exordium has a fatal note of rhetorical exaggeration, not because the kind of passion is impossible, but because Shelley does not convince us that in this instance he had really been its subject.   His own critique, following so close upon the publication of *Epipsychidion,* confirms the impression made by it, and justifies the conclusion that he had utilized his feeling for Emilia to express a favourite doctrine in impassioned verse.

To students of Shelley's inner life *Epipsychidion* will always have high value, independently of its beauty of style, as containing his doctrine of love. It is the full expression of the esoteric principle presented to us in *Alastor*, the *Hymn to Intellectual Beauty*, and *Prince Athanase*. But the words just quoted, which may be compared with Mrs. Shelley's note to *Prince Athanase*, authorize our pointing out what he himself recognized as the defect of his theory. Instead of remaining true to the conception of Beauty expressed in the *Hymn*, Shelley " sought through the world the One whom he may love." Thus, while his doctrine in *Epipsychidion* seems Platonic, it will not square with the *Symposium*. Plato treats the love of a beautiful person as a mere initiation into divine mysteries, the first step in the ladder that ascends to heaven. When a man has formed a just conception of the universal beauty, he looks back with a smile upon those who find their soul's sphere in the love of some mere mortal object. Tested by this standard, Shelley's identification of Intellectual Beauty with so many daughters of earth, and his worshipping love of Emilia, is a spurious Platonism. Plato would have said that to seek the Idea of Beauty in Emilia Viviani was a retrogressive step. All that she could do, would be to quicken the soul's sense of beauty, to stir it from its lethargy, and to make it divine the eternal reality of beauty in the supersensual world of thought. This Shelley had already acknowledged in the *Hymn;* and this he emphasizes in these words :—" The error consists in seeking in a mortal image the likeness of what is, perhaps, eternal."

The fragments and cancelled passages published in Forman's edition do not throw much light upon *Epipsy-*

chidion. The longest, entitled *To his Genius* by its first
editor, Mr. Garnett, reads like the induction to a poem
conceived and written in a different key, and at a lower
level of inspiration. It has, however, this extraordinary
interest that it deals with a love which is both love and
friendship, above sex, spiritual, unintelligible to the
world at large. Thus the fragment enables the student
better to realize the kind of worship so passionately expressed in *Epipsychidion.*

The news of Keats's death at Rome on the 27th of
December, 1820, and the erroneous belief that it had been
accelerated, if not caused, by a contemptible review of
Endymion in the *Quarterly*, stirred Shelley to the composition of *Adonais.* He had it printed at Pisa, and sent
copies to Ollier for circulation in London. This poem
was a favourite with its author, who hoped not only that
it might find acceptance with the public, but also that it
would confer lustre upon the memory of a poet whom he
sincerely admired. No criticisms upon Shelley's works
are half so good as his own. It is, therefore, interesting to
collect the passages in which he speaks of an elegy only
equalled in our language by *Lycidas*, and in the point of passionate eloquence even superior to Milton's youthful lament
for his friend. " The *Adonais*, in spite of its mysticism," he
writes to Ollier, " is the least imperfect of my compositions."
" I confess I should be surprised if that poem were born to
an immortality of oblivion." " It is a highly wrought *piece
of art*, and perhaps better, in point of composition, than
anything I have written." " It is absurd in any review to
criticize *Adonais*, and still more to pretend that the verses
are bad." " I know what to think of *Adonais*, but what
to think of those who confound it with the many bad
poems of the day, I know not." Again, alluding to the

stanzas hurled against the infamous *Quarterly* reviewer, he says :—" I have dipped my pen in consuming fire for his destroyers ; otherwise the style is calm and solemn."

With these estimates the reader of to-day will cordially agree. Although *Adonais* is not so utterly beyond the scope of other poets as *Prometheus* or *Epipsychidion*, it presents Shelley's qualities in a form of even and sustained beauty, brought within the sphere of the dullest apprehensions. Shelley, we may notice, dwells upon the *art* of the poem ; and this, perhaps, is what at first sight will strike the student most. He chose as a foundation for his work those laments of Bion for Adonis, and of Moschus for Bion, which aret he most pathetic products of Greek idyllic poetry ; and the transmutation of their material into the substance of highly spiritualized modern thought, reveals the potency of a Prospero's wand. It is a metamorphosis whereby the art of excellent but positive poets has been translated into the sphere of metaphysical imagination. Urania takes the place of Aphrodite ; the thoughts and fancies and desires of the dead singer are substituted for Bion's cupids ; and instead of mountain shepherds, the living bards of England are summoned to lament around the poet's bier. Yet it is only when Shelley frees himself from the influence of his models, that he soars aloft on mighty wing. This point too, is the point of transition from death, sorrow, and the past to immortality, joy, and the rapture of the things that cannot pass away. The first and second portions of the poem are, at the same time, thoroughly concordant, and the passage from the one to the other is natural. Two quotations from *Adonais* will suffice to show the power and sweetness of its verse.

The first is a description of Shelley himself following Byron and Moore—the " Pilgrim of Eternity," and Ierne's

" sweetest lyrist of her saddest wrong"—to the couch where
Keats lies dead. There is both pathos and unconscious
irony in his making these two poets the chief mourners,
when we remember what Byron wrote about Keats in
Don Juan, and what Moore afterwards recorded of Shelley;
and when we think, moreover, how far both Keats and
Shelley have outsoared Moore, and disputed with Byron
his supreme place in the heaven of poetry.

> Midst others of less note, came one frail Form,
> A phantom among men, companionless
> As the last cloud of an expiring storm,
> Whose thunder is its knell. He, as I guess,
> Had gazed on Nature's naked loveliness,
> Actæon-like, and now he fled astray
> With feeble steps o'er the world's wilderness,
> And his own thoughts, along that rugged way,
> Pursued like raging hounds their father and their prey.

> A pard-like Spirit beautiful and swift—
> A Love in desolation masked—a Power
> Girt round with weakness ; it can scarce uplift
> The weight of the superincumbent hour ;
> It is a dying lamp, a falling shower,
> A breaking billow ;—even whilst we speak
> Is it not broken ? On the withering flower
> The killing sun smiles brightly : on a cheek
> The life can burn in blood, even while the heart may break.

> His head was bound with pansies over-blown,
> And faded violets, white and pied and blue ;
> And a light spear topped with a cypress cone,
> Round whose rude shaft dark ivy-tresses grew
> Yet dripping with the forest's noon-day dew,
> Vibrated, as the ever-beating heart
> Shook the weak hand that grasped it. Of that crew
> He came the last, neglected and apart ;
> A herd-abandoned deer, struck by the hunter's dart.

The second passage is the peroration of the poem. Nowhere has Shelley expressed his philosophy of man's re-

lation to the universe with more sublimity and with a more imperial command of language than in these stanzas. If it were possible to identify that philosophy with any recognized system of thought, it might be called pantheism. But it is difficult to affix a name, stereotyped by the usage of the schools, to the aerial spiritualism of its ardent and impassioned poet's creed.

The movement of the long melodious sorrow-song has just been interrupted by three stanzas, in which Shelley lashes the reviewer of Keats. He now bursts forth afresh into the music of consolation :—

> Peace, peace ! he is not dead, he doth not sleep !
> He hath awakened from the dream of life.
> 'Tis we who, lost in stormy visions, keep
> With phantoms an unprofitable strife,
> And in mad trance strike with our spirit's knife
> Invulnerable nothings.   *We* decay
> Like corpses in a charnel ; fear and grief
> Convulse us and consume us day by day,
> And cold hopes swarm like worms within our living clay.

> He has outsoared the shadow of our night ;
> Envy and calumny, and hate and pain,
> And that unrest which men miscall delight,
> Can touch him not and torture not again ;
> From the contagion of the world's slow stain
> He is secure, and now can never mourn
> A heart grown cold, a head grown grey in vain ;
> Nor, when the spirit's self has ceased to burn,
> With sparkless ashes load an unlamented urn.

> He lives, he wakes—'tis Death is dead, not he ;
> Mourn not for Adonais.—Thou young Dawn,
> Turn all thy dew to splendour, for from thee
> The spirit thou lamentest is not gone ;
> Ye caverns and ye forests, cease to moan !
> Cease, ye faint flowers and fountains, and thou Air
> Which like a mourning veil thy scarf hadst thrown
> O'er the abandoned Earth, now leave it bare
> Even to the joyous stars which smile on its despair !

He is made one with Nature : there is heard
His voice in all her music, from the moan
Of thunder, to the song of night's sweet bird ;
He is a presence to be felt and known
In darkness and in light, from herb and stone,
Spreading itself where'er that Power may move
Which has withdrawn his being to its own ;
  Which wields the world with never wearied love,
Sustains it from beneath, and kindles it above.

He is a portion of the loveliness
Which once he made more lovely : he doth bear
His part, while the One Spirit's plastic stress
Sweeps through the dull dense world, compelling there
All new successions to the forms they wear ;
Torturing th' unwilling dross that checks its flight
To its own likeness, as each mass may bear ;
  And bursting in its beauty and its might
From trees and beasts and men into the Heaven's light.

But the absorption of the human soul into primeval
nature-forces, the blending of the principle of thought
with the universal spirit of beauty, is not enough to
satisfy man's yearning after immortality. Therefore in the
next three stanzas the indestructibility of the personal
self is presented to us, as the soul of Adonais passes into
the company of the illustrious dead who, like him, were
untimely slain :—

The splendours of the firmament of time
May be eclipsed, but are extinguished not :
Like stars to their appointed height they climb,
And death is a low mist which cannot blot
The brightness it may veil. When lofty thought
Lifts a young heart above its mortal lair,
And love and life contend in it, for what
  Shall be its earthly doom, the dead live there,
And move like winds of light on dark and stormy air.

> The inheritors of unfulfilled renown
> Rose from their thrones, built beyond mortal thought,
> Far in the Unapparent. Chatterton
> Rose pale, his solemn agony had not
> Yet faded from him; Sidney, as he fought
> And as he fell and as he lived and loved,
> Sublimely mild, a Spirit without spot,
> Arose; and Lucan, by his death approved :—
> Oblivion as they rose, shrank like a thing reproved.
>
> And many more, whose names on Earth are dark,
> But whose transmitted effluence cannot die
> So long as fire outlives the parent spark,
> Rose, robed in dazzling immortality.
> " Thou art become as one of us," they cry ;
> " It was for thee yon kingless sphere has long
> Swung blind in unascended majesty,
> Silent alone amid an Heaven of song.
> Assume thy wingèd throne, thou Vesper of our throng ! "

From the more universal and philosophical aspects of
his theme, the poet once more turns to the special subject
that had stirred him. Adonais lies dead ; and those who
mourn him, must seek his grave. He has escaped : to
follow him is to die ; and where should we learn to dote
on death unterrified, if not in Rome ? In this way the
description of Keats's resting-place beneath the pyramid
of Cestius, which was also destined to be Shelley's own,
is introduced :—

> Who mourns for Adonais ? oh come forth,
> Fond wretch ! and show thyself and him aright.
> Clasp with thy panting soul the pendulous Earth ;
> As from a centre, dart thy spirit's light
> Beyond all worlds, until its spacious might
> Satiate the void circumference : then shrink
> Even to a point within our day and night ;
> And keep thy heart light, let it make thee sink
> When hope has kindled hope, and lured thee to the brink.

Or go to Rome, which is the sepulchre,
Oh, not of him, but of our joy: 'tis nought
That ages, empires, and religions there
Lie buried in the ravage they have wrought;
For such as he can lend,—they borrow not
Glory from those who made the world their prey;
And he is gathered to the kings of thought
Who waged contention with their time's decay,
And of the past are all that cannot pass away.

Go thou to Rome,—at once the Paradise,
The grave, the city, and the wilderness;
And where its wrecks like shattered mountains rise,
And flowering weeds and fragrant copses dress
The bones of Desolation's nakedness,
Pass, till the Spirit of the spot shall lead
Thy footsteps to a slope of green access,
Where, like an infant's smile, over the dead
A light of laughing flowers along the grass is spread;

And grey walls moulder round, on which dull Time
Feeds, like slow fire upon a hoary brand;
And one keen pyramid with wedge sublime,
Pavilioning the dust of him who planned
This refuge for his memory, doth stand
Like flame transformed to marble; and beneath,
A field is spread, on which a newer band
Have pitched in Heaven's smile their camp of death,
Welcoming him we lose with scarce extinguished breath.

Here pause: these graves are all too young as yet
To have outgrown the sorrow which consigned
Its charge to each; and if the seal is set,
Here, on one fountain of a mourning mind,
Break it not thou! too surely shalt thou find
Thine own well full, if thou returnest home,
Of tears and gall.   From the world's bitter wind
Seek shelter in the shadow of the tomb.
What Adonais is, why fear we to become?

Yet again the thought of Death as the deliverer, the
revealer, and the mystagogue, through whom the soul of

man is reunited to the spirit of the universe, returns ;
and on this solemn note the poem closes. The symphony
of exultation which had greeted the passage of Adonais
into the eternal world, is here subdued to a graver key,
as befits the mood of one whom mystery and mourning
still oppress on earth. Yet even in the somewhat less
than jubilant conclusion we feel that highest of all
Shelley's qualities—the liberation of incalculable energies,
the emancipation and expansion of a force within the soul,
victorious over circumstance, exhilarated and elevated by
contact with such hopes as make a feebler spirit tremble:

> The One remains, the many change and pass ;
> Heaven's light for ever shines, Earth's shadows fly ;
> Life, like a dome of many-coloured glass,
> Stains the white radiance of Eternity,
> Until Death tramples it to fragments.—Die,
> If thou wouldst be with that which thou dost seek !
> Follow where all is fled !—Rome's azure sky,
> Flowers, ruins, statues, music, words, are weak
> The glory they transfuse with fitting truth to speak.

> Why linger, why turn back, why shrink, my Heart ?
> Thy hopes are gone before : from all things here
> They have departed ; thou shouldst now depart !
> A light is past from the revolving year,
> And man and woman ; and what still is dear
> Attracts to crush, repels to make thee wither.
> The soft sky smiles, the low wind whispers near :
> 'Tis Adonais calls ! oh, hasten thither!
> No more let Life divide what Death can join together.

> That light whose smile kindles the Universe,
> That beauty in which all things work and move,
> That benediction which the eclipsing curse
> Of birth can quench not, that sustaining Love
> Which through the web of being blindly wove

By man and beast and earth and air and sea,
Burns bright or dim, as each are mirrors of
The fire for which all thirst, now beams on me,
Consuming the last clouds of cold mortality.

The breath whose might I have invoked in song
Descends on me; my spirit's bark is driven
Far from the shore, far from the trembling throng
Whose sails were never to the tempest given.
The massy earth and spherèd skies are riven!
I am borne darkly, fearfully afar;
Whilst burning through the inmost veil of Heaven,
The soul of Adonais, like a star,
Beacons from the abode where the Eternal are.

It will be seen that whatever Shelley may from time to time have said about the immortality of the soul, he was no materialist, and no believer in the extinction of the spiritual element by death. Yet he was too wise to dogmatize upon a problem which by its very nature admits of no solution in this world. "I hope," he said, "but my hopes are not unmixed with fear for what will befall this inestimable spirit when we appear to die." On another occasion he told Trelawny: "I am content to see no farther into futurity than Plato and Bacon. My mind is tranquil; I have no fears and some hopes. In our present gross material state our faculties are clouded; when Death removes our clay coverings, the mystery will be solved." How constantly the thought of death as the revealer was present to his mind, may be gathered from an incident related by Trelawny. They were bathing in the Arno, when Shelley, who could not swim, plunged into deep water, and "lay stretched out at the bottom like a conger eel, not making the least effort or struggle to save himself." Trelawny fished him out, and when he had taken breath, he said: "I always find the bottom of the well,

and they say Truth lies there. In another minute I
should have found it, and you would have found an
empty shell. Death is the veil which those who live call
life ; they sleep, and it is lifted." Yet being pressed by
his friend, he refused to acknowledge a formal and precise
belief in the imperishability of the human soul. "We
know nothing ; we have no evidence ; we cannot express
our inmost thoughts. They are incomprehensible even to
ourselves." The clear insight into the conditions of the
question conveyed by the last sentence is very characteristic
of Shelley. It makes us regret the non-completion of his
essay on a *Future Life*, which would certainly have
stated the problem with rare lucidity and candour, and
would have illuminated the abyss of doubt with a sense
of spiritual realities not often found in combination with
wise suspension of judgment. What he clung to amid all
perplexities, was the absolute and indestructible existence
of the universal as perceived by us in love, beauty, and
delight. Though the destiny of the personal self be
obscure, these things cannot fail. The conclusion of the
Sensitive Plant might be cited as conveying the quintes-
sence of his hope upon this most intangible of riddles.

> Whether the Sensitive Plant, or that
> Which within its boughs like a spirit sat,
> Ere its outward form had known decay,
> Now felt this change, I cannot say.
>
> I dare not guess ; but in this life
> Of error, ignorance, and strife,
> Where nothing is, but all things seem,
> And we the shadows of the dream :
>
> It is a modest creed, and yet
> Pleasant, if one considers it,
> To own that death itself must be,
> Like all the rest, a mockery.

> That garden sweet, that lady fair,
> And all sweet shapes and odours there,
> In truth have never passed away :
> 'Tis we, 'tis ours, are changed ; not they.
>
> For love, and beauty, and delight,
> There is no death nor change ; their might
> Exceeds our organs, which endure
> No light, being themselves obscure.

But it is now time to return from this digression to the
poem which suggested it, and which, more than any other,
serves to illustrate its author's mood of feeling about the
life beyond the grave.   The last lines of *Adonais* might
be read as a prophecy of his own death by drowning.   The
frequent recurrence of this thought in his poetry is, to say
the least, singular.   In *Alastor* we read :—

> A restless impulse urged him to embark
> And meet lone Death on the drear ocean's waste ;
> For well he knew that mighty Shadow loves
> The slimy caverns of the populous deep.

The *Ode to Liberty* closes on the same note :—

> As a far taper fades with fading night ;
> As a brief insect dies with dying day,
> My song, its pinions disarrayed of might,
> Drooped.   O'er it closed the echoes far away
> Of the great voice which did its flight sustain,
> As waves which lately paved his watery way
> Hiss round a drowner's head in their tempestuous play.

The *Stanzas written in Dejection, near Naples,* echo the
thought with a slight variation :—

> Yet now despair itself is mild,
> Even as the winds and waters are ;
> I could lie down like a tired child,
> And weep away the life of care

Which I have borne, and yet must bear,—
Till death like sleep might steal on me,
And I might feel in the warm air
My cheek grow cold, and hear the sea
Breathe o'er my dying brain its last monotony.

Trelawny tells a story of his friend's life at Lerici, which
further illustrates his preoccupation with the thought of
death at sea. He took Mrs. Williams and her children out
upon the bay in his little boat one afternoon, and starting
suddenly from a deep reverie, into which he had fallen,
exclaimed with a joyful and resolute voice, " Now let us
together solve the great mystery !" Too much value must
not be attached to what might have been a mere caprice
of utterance. Yet the proposal not unreasonably fright-
ened Mrs. Williams, for Shelley's friends were accustomed to expect the realization of his wildest fancies. It
may incidentally be mentioned that before the water finally
claimed its victim, he had often been in peril of life upon
his fatal element—during the first voyage to Ireland,
while crossing the Channel with Mary in an open boat,
again at Meillerie with Byron, and once at least with
Williams.

A third composition of the year 1821 was inspired by the
visit of Prince Mavrocordato to Pisa. He called on Shelley
in April, showed him a copy of Prince Ipsilanti's proclama-
tion, and announced that Greece was determined to strike
a blow for freedom. The news aroused all Shelley's
enthusiasm, and he began the lyrical drama of *Hellas*,
which he has described as "a sort of imitation of the
Persae of Æschylus." We find him at work upon it in
October; and it must have been finished by the end of
that month, since the dedication bears the date of November 1st, 1821. Shelley did not set great store by it.

" It was written," he says, " without much care, and in
one of those few moments of enthusiasm which now
seldom visit me, and which make me pay dear for their
visits." The preface might, if space permitted, be cited
as a specimen of his sound and weighty judgment upon
one of the greatest political questions of this century.
What he says about the debt of the modern world
to ancient Hellas, is no less pregnant than his severe
strictures upon the part played by Russia in dealing
with Eastern questions. For the rest, the poem is
distinguished by passages of great lyrical beauty, rising
at times to the sublimest raptures, and closing on the
half-pathetic cadence of that well-known Chorus, " The
world's great age begins anew." Of dramatic interest
it has but little ; nor is the play, as finished, equal to
the promise held forth by the superb fragment of its
so-called Prologue.[1] This truly magnificent torso must,
I think, have been the commencement of the drama as
conceived upon a different and more colossal plan, which
Shelley rejected for some unknown reason. It shows the
influence not only of the Book of Job, but also of the
Prologue in Heaven to Faust, upon his mind.

The lyric movement of the Chorus from *Hellas*, which
I propose to quote, marks the highest point of Shelley's
rhythmical invention. As for the matter expressed in it,
we must not forget that these stanzas are written for a
Chorus of Greek captive women, whose creed does not pre-
vent their feeling a regret for the " mightier forms of an
older, austerer worship." Shelley's note reminds the
reader, with characteristic caution and frankness, that
" the popular notions of Christianity are represented in
this Chorus as true in their relation to the worship they

[1] Forman, iv. p. 95.

superseded, and that which in all probability they will
supersede, without considering their merits in a relation
more universal."

> Worlds on worlds are rolling ever
>   From creation to decay,
> Like the bubbles on a river
>   Sparkling, bursting, borne away.
>   But they are still immortal
>   Who, through birth's orient portal,
> And death's dark chasm hurrying to and fro,
>   Clothe their unceasing flight
>   In the brief dust and light
> Gathered around their chariots as they go ;
>   New shapes they still may weave,
>   New gods, new laws receive ;
> Bright or dim are they, as the robes they last
>   On Death's bare ribs had cast.
>
>
>   A power from the unknown.God,
>   A Promethean conqueror came ;
> Like a triumphal path he trod
>   The thorns of death and shame.
>   A mortal shape to him
>   Was like the vapour dim
> Which the orient planet animates with light.
>   Hell, Sin, and Slavery came,
>   Like bloodhounds mild and tame,
> Nor preyed until their Lord had taken flight.
>   The moon of Mahomet
>   Arose, and it shall set :
> While blazoned as on heaven's immortal noon
>   The cross leads generations on.
>
>
>   Swift as the radiant shapes of sleep
>   From one whose dreams are paradise,
>   Fly, when the fond wretch wakes to weep,
>   And day peers forth with her blank eyes ;
>   So fleet, so faint, so fair,
>   The Powers of earth and air

Fled from the folding star of Bethlehem:
    Apollo, Pan, and Love,
    And even Olympian Jove
Grew weak, for killing Truth had glared on them.
    Our hills, and seas, and streams,
    Dispeopled of their dreams,
Their waters turned to blood, their dew to tears,
    Wailed for the golden years.

In the autumn of this year Shelley paid Lord Byron a
visit at Ravenna, where he made acquaintance with the
Countess Guiccioli. It was then settled that Byron, who
had formed the project of starting a journal to be called
The Liberal in concert with Leigh Hunt, should himself
settle in Pisa. Leigh Hunt was to join his brother poets
in the same place. The prospect gave Shelley great pleasure, for he was sincerely attached to Hunt; and though
he would not promise contributions to the journal, partly
lest his name should bring discredit on it, and partly
because he did not choose to appear before the world as a
hanger-on of Byron's, he thoroughly approved of a plan
which would be profitable to his friend by bringing him
into close relation with the most famous poet of the age.[1]
That he was not without doubts as to Byron's working
easily in harness with Leigh Hunt, may be seen in his
correspondence; and how fully these doubts were destined
to be confirmed, is only too well known.

At Ravenna he was tormented by the report of some
more than usually infamous calumny. What it was, we do
not know; but that it made profound impression on his
mind, appears from a remarkable letter addressed to his
wife on the 16th and 17th of August from Ravenna. In
it he repeats his growing weariness, and his wish to escape

---

[1] See the Letter to Leigh Hunt, Pisa, Aug. 26, 1821.

from society to solitude; the weariness of a nature
wounded and disappointed by commerce with the world,
but neither soured nor driven to fury by cruel wrongs.
It is noticeable at the same time that he clings to his
present place of residence :—" our roots never struck so
deeply as at Pisa, and the transplanted tree flourishes not."
At Pisa he had found real rest and refreshment in the
society of his two friends, the Williamses.   Some of his
saddest and most touching lyrics of this year are addressed
to Jane—for so Mrs. Williams was called ; and attentive
students may perceive that the thought of Emilia was
already blending by subtle transitions with the new thought
of Jane.   One poem, almost terrible in its intensity of
melancholy, is hardly explicable on the supposition that
Shelley was quite happy in his home.[1]   These words must
be taken as implying no reflection either upon Mary's love
for him, or upon his own power to bear the slighter
troubles of domestic life.   He was not a spoiled child of
fortune, a weak egotist, or a querulous complainer.   But
he was always seeking and never finding the satisfaction
of some deeper craving.   In his own words, he had loved
Antigone before he visited this earth : and no one woman
could probably have made him happy, because he was for
ever demanding more from love than it can give in the
mixed circumstances of mortal life.   Moreover, it must
be remembered that his power of self-expression has
bestowed permanent form on feelings which may have been
but transitory ; nor can we avoid the conclusion that,
sincere as Shelley was, he, like all poets, made use of the
emotion of the moment for purposes of art, converting an
ephemeral mood into something typical and universal.   This
was almost certainly the case with *Epipsychidion.*

[1] " The Serpent is shut out from Paradise."

So much at any rate had to be said upon this subject ; for careful readers of Shelley's minor poems are forced to the conviction that during the last year of his life he often found relief from a wretchedness, which, however real, can hardly be defined, in the sympathy of this true-hearted woman. The affection he felt for Jane was beyond question pure and honourable. All the verses he addressed to her, passed through her husband's hands without the slightest interruption to their intercourse ; and Mrs. Shelley, who was not unpardonably jealous of her Ariel, continued to be Mrs. Williams's warm friend. A passage from Shelley's letter of June 18, 1822, expresses the plain prose of his relation to the Williamses :—" They are people who are very pleasing to me. But words are not the instruments of our intercourse. I like Jane more and more, and I find Williams the most amiable of companions. She has a taste for music, and an eloquence of form and motions that compensate in some degree for the lack of literary refinement."

Two lyrics of this period may here be introduced, partly for the sake of their intrinsic beauty, and partly because they illustrate the fecundity of Shelley's genius during the months of tranquil industry which he passed at Pisa. The first is an Invocation to Night :—

> Swiftly walk over the western wave,
>   Spirit of Night !
> Out of the misty eastern cave,
> Where all the long and lone daylight,
> Thou wovest dreams of joy and fear,
> Which make thee terrible and dear,—
>   Swift be thy flight !
>
> Wrap thy form in a mantle grey,
>   Star-inwrought !
> Blind with thine hair the eyes of day,

Kiss her until she be wearied out.
Then wander o'er city, and sea, and land,
Touching all with thine opiate wand—
            Come, long-sought !

When I arose and saw the dawn,
            I sighed for thee ;
When light rode high, and the dew was gone,
And noon lay heavy on flower and tree,
And the weary Day turned to his rest,
Lingering like an unloved guest,
            I sighed for thee.

Thy brother Death came, and cried,
            " Wouldst thou me ? "
Thy sweet child Sleep, the filmy-eyed,
Murmured like a noon-tide bee,
" Shall I nestle near thy side ?
Wouldst thou me ? "—And I replied,
            " No, not thee ! "

Death will come when thou art dead,
            Soon, too soon—
Sleep will come when thou art fled ;
Of neither would I ask the boon
I ask of thee, beloved Night—
Swift be thine approaching flight,
            Come soon, soon !

The second is an Epithalamium composed for a drama
which his friend Williams was writing.   Students of the
poetic art will find it not uninteresting to compare the
three versions of this Bridal Song, given by Mr. Forman.[5]
They prove that Shelley was no careless writer.

The golden gates of sleep unbar
    Where strength and beauty, met together,
Kindle their image like a star
    In a sea of glassy weather !

---

[1] Vol. iv. p. 89.

Night, with all thy stars look down—
Darkness, weep thy holiest dew!
Never smiled the inconstant moon
　　On a pair so true.
Let eyes not see their own delight;
Haste, swift Hour, and thy flight
　　Oft renew.

Fairies, sprites, and angels, keep her!
Holy stars, permit no wrong!
And return to wake the sleeper,
　　Dawn, ere it be long.
O joy! O fear! what will be done
In the absence of the sun!
　　Come along!

Lyrics like these, delicate in thought and exquisitely
finished in form, were produced with a truly wonderful
profusion in this season of his happiest fertility. A
glance at the last section of Mr. Palgrave's *Golden Treasury*
shows how large a place they occupy among the permanent
jewels of our literature.

The month of January added a new and most important member to the little Pisan circle. This was
Captain Edward John Trelawny, to whom more than to
any one else but Hogg and Mrs. Shelley, the students of
the poet's life are indebted for details at once accurate
and characteristic. Trelawny had lived a free life in all
quarters of the globe, far away from literary cliques and
the society of cities, in contact with the sternest realities
of existence, which had developed his self-reliance and
his physical qualities to the utmost. The impression,
therefore, made on him by Shelley has to be gravely esti-
mated by all who still incline to treat the poet as a patho-
logical specimen of humanity. This true child of nature
recognized in his new friend far more than in Byron the

M

stuff of a real man. "To form a just idea of his poetry,
you should have witnessed his daily life ; his words and
actions best illustrated his writings." "The cynic Byron
acknowledged him to be the best and ablest man he had
ever known. The truth was, Shelley loved everything
better than himself." "I have seen Shelley and Byron in
society, and the contrast was as marked as their characters.
The former, not thinking of himself, was as much at ease as
in his own home, omitting no occasion of obliging those
whom he came in contact with, readily conversing with
all or any who addressed him, irrespective of age or rank,
dress or address." "All who heard him felt the charm
of his simple, earnest manner : while Byron knew him
to be exempt from the egotism, pedantry, coxcombry, and
more than all the rivalry of authorship." "Shelley's
mental activity was infectious ; he kept your brain in
constant action." "He was always in earnest." "He
never laid aside his book and magic mantle ; he waved
his wand, and Byron, after a faint show of defiance, stood
mute. . . . . Shelley's earnestness and just criticism held
him captive." These sentences, and many others, prove
that Trelawny, himself somewhat of a cynic, cruelly
exposing false pretensions, and detesting affectation in
any form, paid unreserved homage to the heroic qualities
this "dreamy bard,"—"uncommonly awkward," as he
also called him—bad rider and poor seaman as he was
—"over-sensitive," and "eternally brooding on his own
thoughts," who "had seen no more of the waking-day than
a girl at a boarding-school." True to himself, gentle,
tender, with the courage of a lion, "frank and outspoken,
like a well-conditioned boy, well-bred and considerate for
others, because he was totally devoid of selfishness and
vanity," Shelley seemed to this unprejudiced companion

of his last few months that very rare product for which
Diogenes searched in vain—a man.

Their first meeting must be told in Trelawny's own
words—words no less certain of immortality than the
fame of him they celebrate. "The Williamses received
me in their earnest, cordial manner; we had a great deal
to communicate to each other, and were in loud and
animated conversation, when I was rather put out by
observing in the passage near the open door, opposite to
where I sat, a pair of glittering eyes steadily fixed on
mine; it was too dark to make out whom they belonged
to. With the acuteness of a woman, Mrs. Williams's
eyes followed the direction of mine, and going to the
doorway she laughingly said, 'Come in, Shelley, it's only
our friend Tre just arrived.' Swiftly gliding in, blush-
ing like a girl, a tall, thin stripling held out both his
hands; and although I could hardly believe, as I looked
at his flushed, feminine, and artless face, that it could be
the poet, I returned his warm pressure. After the ordinary greetings and courtesies he sat down and listened.
I was silent from astonishment: was it possible this mild-
looking, beardless boy, could be the veritable monster at
war with all the world?—excommunicated by the Fathers
of the Church, deprived of his civil rights by the fiat of a
grim Lord Chancellor, discarded by every member of his
family, and denounced by the rival sages of our literature
as the founder of a Satanic school? I could not believe it;
it must be a hoax. He was habited like a boy, in a black
jacket and trousers, which he seemed to have outgrown, or
his tailor, as is the custom, had most shamefully stinted
him in his 'sizings.' Mrs. Williams saw my embarrass-
ment, and to relieve me asked Shelley what book he had in
his hand? His face brightened, and he answered briskly,—

" ' Calderon's *Magico Prodigioso*—I am translating some passages in it.'

" ' Oh, read it to us.'

" Shoved off from the shore of commonplace incidents that could not interest him, and fairly launched on a theme that did, he instantly became oblivious of everything but the book in his hand. The masterly manner in which he analysed the genius of the author, his lucid interpretation of the story, and the ease with which he translated into our language the most subtle and imaginative passages of the Spanish poet, were marvellous, as was his command of the two languages. After this touch of his quality I no longer doubted his identity; a dead silence ensued; looking up, I asked,—

" ' Where is he ? '

" Mrs. Williams said, ' Who ? Shelley ? Oh, he comes and goes like a spirit, no one knows when or where.' "

Two little incidents which happened in the winter of 1821-2 deserve to be recorded. News reached the Pisan circle early in December that a man who had insulted the Host at Lucca, was sentenced to be burned. Shelley proposed that the English—himself, Byron, Medwin, and their friend Mr. Taafe—should immediately arm and ride off to rescue him. The scheme took Byron's fancy; but they agreed to try less Quixotic measures before they had recourse to force, and their excitement was calmed by hearing that the man's sentence had been commuted to the galleys. The other affair brought them less agreeably into contact with the Tuscan police. The party were riding home one afternoon in March, when a mounted dragoon came rushing by, breaking their ranks and nearly unhorsing Mr. Taafe. Byron and Shelley rode after him to remonstrate; but the man struck Shelley from his saddle with a sabre blow. The English then pursued him into Pisa, making such a clatter that one of Byron's servants issued with a pitchfork from the Casa Lanfranchi, and wounded the fellow somewhat seriously, under the impression that it was necessary to defend his master. Shelley called the whole matter "a trifling piece of business;" but it was strictly investigated by the authorities; and though the dragoon was found to have been in the wrong, Byron had to retire for a season to Leghorn. Another consequence was the exile of Count Gamba and his father from Tuscany, which led to Byron's final departure from Pisa.

The even current of Shelley's life was not often broken by such adventures. Trelawny gives the following account of how he passed his days : he "was up at six or seven, reading Plato, Sophocles, or Spinoza, with the accompaniment of a hunch of dry bread ; then he joined Williams in a sail on the Arno, in a flat-bottomed skiff, book in hand, and from thence he went to the pine-forest, or some out-of-the-way place. When the birds went to roost he returned home, and talked and read until midnight." The great wood of stone pines on the Pisan Maremma was his favourite study. Trelawny tells us how he found him there alone one day, and in what state was the MS. of that prettiest lyric, *Ariel, to Miranda take.* "It was a frightful scrawl ; words smeared out with his finger, and one upon the other, over and over in tiers, and all run together in most 'admired disorder ;' it might have been taken for a sketch of a marsh overgrown with bulrushes, and the blots for wild ducks ; such a dashed-off daub as self-conceited artists mistake for a manifestation of genius. On my observing this to him, he answered, ' When my brain gets heated with thought, it soon boils, and throws off images and words faster than I can skim them off. In the

morning, when cooled down, out of the rude sketch as
you justly call it, I shall attempt a drawing.'"

A daily visit to Byron diversified existence. Byron
talked more sensibly with Shelley than with his commonplace acquaintances; and when he began to gossip,
Shelley retired into his own thoughts. Then they
would go pistol-shooting, Byron's trembling hand con-
trasting with his friend's firmness. They had invented a "little language" for this sport: firing was
called *tiring*; hitting, *colping*; missing, *mancating*, &c.
It was in fact a kind of pigeon Italian. Shelley acquired
two nick-names in the circle of his Pisan friends, both
highly descriptive. He was Ariel and the Snake. The
latter suited him because of his noiseless gliding movement,
bright eyes and ethereal diet. It was first given to him by
Byron during a reading of *Faust*. When he came to the
line of Mephistophiles, "Wie meine Muhme, die berühmte
Schlange" and translated it, "My aunt, the renowned
Snake," Byron cried, "Then you are her nephew."
Shelley by no means resented the epithet. Indeed he
alludes to it in his letters and in a poem already referred to
above.

Soon after Trelawny's arrival the party turned their
thoughts to nautical affairs. Shelley had already done a
good deal of boating with Williams on the Arno and the
Serchio, and had on one occasion nearly lost his life by
the capsizing of their tiny craft. They now determined
to build a larger yacht for excursions on the sea; while
Byron, liking the project of a summer residence upon the
Bay of Spezia, made up his mind to have one too.
Shelley's was to be an open boat carrying sail, Byron's, a
large decked schooner. The construction of both was
entrusted to a Genoese builder, under the direction of

Trelawny's friend, Captain Roberts. Such was the birth of
the ill-fated *Don Juan*, which cost the lives of Shelley and
Williams, and of the *Bolivar*, which carried Byron off to
Genoa bofore he finally set sail for Greece. Captain Roberts
was allowed to have his own way about the latter; but
Shelley and Williams had set their hearts upon a model for
their little yacht, which did not suit the Captain's notions
of sea-worthiness. Williams overruled his objections, and
the *Don Juan* was built according to his cherished fancy.
" When it was finished," says Trelawny, " it took two tons
of iron ballast to bring her down to her bearings, and then
she was very crank in a breeze, though not deficient in
beam. She was fast, strongly built, and Torbay rigged."
She was christened by Lord Byron, not wholly with Shelley's approval; and one young English sailor, Charles
Vivian, in addition to Williams and Shelley, formed her
crew. " It was great fun," says Trelawny, " to witness
Williams teaching the poet how to steer, and other points
of seamanship. As usual, Shelley had a book in hand,
saying he could read and steer at the same time, as one
was mental, the other mechanical." " The boy was quick
and handy, and used to boats. Williams was not as
deficient as I anticipated, but over-anxious, and wanted
practice, which alone makes a man prompt in emergency.
Shelley was intent on catching images from the ever-
changing sea and sky, he heeded not the boat."

CHAPTER VII.

LAST DAYS.

THE advance of spring made the climate of Pisa too hot for comfort; and early in April Trelawny and Williams rode off to find a suitable lodging for themselves and the Shelleys on the Gulf of Spezia. They pitched upon a house called the Villa Magni, between Lerici and San Terenzio, which " looked more like a boat or bathing-house than a place to live in. It consisted of a terrace or ground-floor un-paved, and used for storing boat-gear and fishing-tackle, and of a single storey over it, divided into a hall or saloon and four small rooms, which had once been white-washed; there was one chimney for cooking. This place we thought the Shelleys might put up with for the summer. The only good thing about it was a verandah facing the sea, and almost over it." When it came to be inhabited, the central hall was used for the living and eating room of the whole party. The Shelleys occupied two rooms facing each other; the Williamses had one of the remaining chambers, and Trelawny another. Access to these smaller apartments could only be got through the saloon; and this circumstance once gave rise to a ludicrous incident, when Shelley, having lost his clothes out bathing, had to cross, *in puris naturalibus*, not undetected, though covered in his retreat by the clever Italian handmaiden, through a luncheon party assembled in the dining-room. The horror of the ladies at the poet's unexpected apparition and his innocent self-defence are well described by Trelawny. Life in the villa was of the simplest description. To get food was no easy matter; and the style of the furniture may be guessed by Trelawny's laconic remark that the sea was his only washing-basin.

They arrived at Villa Magni on the 26th of April, and began a course of life which was not interrupted till the final catastrophe of July 8. These few weeks were in many respects the happiest of Shelley's life. We seem to discern in his last letter of importance, recently edited by Mr. Garnett, that he was now conscious of having reached a platform from which he could survey his past achievement, and whence he would probably have risen to a loftier altitude, by a calmer and more equable exercise of powers which had been ripening during the last three years of life in Italy. Meanwhile, "I am content," he writes, "if the heaven above me is calm for the passing moment." And this tranquillity was perfect, with none of the oppressive sense of coming danger, which distinguishes the calm before a storm. He was far away from the distractions of the world he hated, in a scene of indescribable beauty, among a population little removed from the state of savages, who enjoyed the primitive pleasures of a race at one with nature, and toiled with hardy perseverance on the element he loved so well. His company was thoroughly congenial and well mixed. He spent his days in excursions on the water with Williams, or in solitary musings in his cranky little skiff, floating upon the shallows in shore, or putting out to sea and waiting for the landward breeze to bring him home. The evenings were passed upon the terrace, listening to Jane's guitar, conversing

with Trelawny, or reading his favourite poets aloud to the
assembled party.

In this delightful solitude, this round of simple occupations, this uninterrupted communion with nature, Shelley's
enthusiasms and inspirations revived with their old strength.
He began a poem, which, if we may judge of its scale by the
fragment we possess, would have been one of the longest, as
it certainly is one of the loftiest of his masterpieces.   The
Triumph of Life is composed in no strain of compliment to the
powers of this world, which quell untameable spirits, and
enslave the noblest by the operation of blind passions and
inordinate ambitions.   It is rather a pageant of the spirit
dragged in chains, led captive to the world, the flesh, and
the devil.   The sonorous march and sultry splendour of the
terza rima stanzas, bearing on their tide of song those multitudes of forms, processionally grand, yet misty with the
dust of their own tramplings, and half-shrouded in a lurid
robe of light, affect the imagination so powerfully that we
are fain to abandon criticism and acknowledge only the
dæmonic fascinations of this solemn mystery.   Some have
compared the *Triumph of Life* to a Panathenaic pomp :
others have found in it a reflex of the burning summer
heat, and blazing sea, and onward undulations of inter-
minable waves, which were the cradle of its maker as he
wrote.   The imagery of Dante plays a part, and Dante has
controlled the structure.   The genius of the Revolution
passes by : Napoleon is there, and Rousseau serves for
guide.   The great of all ages are arraigned, and the spirit
of the world is brought before us, while its heroes pass,
unveil their faces for a moment, and are swallowed in the
throng that has no ending.   But how Shelley meant to
solve the problems he has raised, by what sublime philosophy he purposed to resolve the discords of this revela-

tion more soul-shattering than Daniel's *Mene,* we cannot
even guess. The poem, as we have it, breaks abruptly
with these words : "Then what is Life ? I cried "—a sentence of profoundest import, when we remember that the
questioner was now about to seek its answer in the halls
of Death.

To separate any single passage from a poem which owes
so much of its splendour to the continuity of music and
the succession of visionary images, does it cruel wrong.
Yet this must be attempted; for Shelley is the only
English poet who has successfully handled that most
difficult of metres, *terza rima.* His power over complicated versification cannot be appreciated except by duly
noticing the method he employed in treating a structure
alien, perhaps, to the genius of our literature, and even in
Italian used with perfect mastery by none but Dante. To
select the introduction and part of the first paragraph will
inflict less violence upon the *Triumph of Life* as a whole,
than to detach one of its episodes.

> Swift as a spirit hastening to his task
> Of glory and of good, the Sun sprang forth
> Rejoicing in his splendour, and the mask
>
> Of darkness fell from the awakened Earth.
> The smokeless altars of the mountain snows
> Flamed above crimson clouds, and at the birth
>
> Of light, the Ocean's orison arose,
> To which the birds tempered their matin lay.
> All flowers in field or forest which unclose
>
> Their trembling eyelids to the kiss of day,
> Swinging their censers in the element,
> With orient incense lit by the new ray
>
> Burned slow and inconsumably, and sent
> Their odorous sighs up to the smiling air ;
> And, in succession due, did continent,

Isle, ocean, and all things that in them wear
The form and character of mortal mould,
Rise as the Sun their father rose, to bear

Their portion of the toil, which he of old
Took as his own, and then imposed on them.
But I, whom thoughts which must remain untold

Had kept as wakeful as the stars that gem
The cone of night, now they were laid asleep,
Stretched my faint limbs beneath the hoary stem

Which an old chesnut flung athwart the steep
Of a green Apennine.   Before me fled
The night; behind me rose the day; the deep

Was at my feet, and Heaven above my head,—
When a strange trance over my fancy grew
Which was not slumber, for the shade it spread

Was so transparent that the scene came through
As clear as, when a veil of light is drawn
O'er evening hills, they glimmer; and I knew

That I had felt the freshness of that dawn
Bathe in the same cold dew my brow and hair,
And sate as thus upon that slope of lawn

Under the self-same bough, and heard as there
The birds, the fountains, and the ocean, hold
Sweet talk in music through the enamoured air.
And then a vision on my brain was rolled.

Such is the exordium of the poem.   It will be noticed
that at this point one series of the interwoven triplets is
concluded.   The *Triumph of Life* itself begins with a
new series of rhymes, describing the vision for which pre-
paration has been made in the preceding prelude.   It is
not without perplexity that an ear unaccustomed to the
windings of the *terza rima*, feels its way among them.
Entangled and impeded by the labyrinthine sounds, the

reader might be compared to one who, swimming in his dreams, is carried down the course of a swift river clogged with clinging and retarding water-weeds. He moves; but not without labour: yet after a while the very obstacles add fascination to his movement.

As in that trance of wondrous thought I lay,
This was the tenour of my waking dream :—
Methought I sate beside a public way

Thick strewn with summer dust, and a great stream
Of people there was hurrying to and fro,
Numerous as gnats upon the evening gleam,

All hastening onward, yet none seemed to know
Whither he went, or whence he came, or why
He made one of the multitude, and so

Was borne amid the crowd, as through the sky
One of the million leaves of summer's bier ;
Old age and youth, manhood and infancy,

Mixed in one mighty torrent did appear :
Some flying from the thing they feared, and some
Seeking the object of another's fear ;

And others, as with steps towards the tomb,
Pored on the trodden worms that crawled beneath,
And others mournfully within the gloom

Of their own shadow walked and called it death ;
And some fled from it as it were a ghost,
Half fainting in the affliction of vain breath.

But more, with motions which each other crossed,
Pursued or spurned the shadows the clouds threw,
Or birds within the noon-day ether lost,

Upon that path where flowers never grew,—
And weary with vain toil and faint for thirst,
Heard not the fountains, whose melodious dew

Out of their mossy cells for ever burst;
Nor felt the breeze which from the forest told
Of grassy paths, and wood lawn-interspersed,

With over-arching elms, and caverns cold,
And violet banks where sweet dreams brood ;—but they
Pursued their serious folly as of old.

Here let us break the chain of rhymes that are unbroken
in the text, to notice the extraordinary skill with which
the rhythm has been woven in one paragraph, suggesting
by recurrences of sound the passing of a multitude, which
is presented at the same time to the eye of fancy by
accumulated images.   The next eleven triplets introduce
the presiding genius of the pageant.   Students of Petrarch's
Trionfi will not fail to note what Shelley owes to that
poet, and how he has transmuted the definite imagery of
mediæval symbolism into something metaphysical and
mystic.

And as I gazed, methought that in the way
The throng grew wilder, as the woods of June
When the south wind shakes the extinguished day ;

And a cold glare, intenser than the noon
But icy cold, obscured with blinding light
The sun, as he the stars.   Like the young moon—

When on the sunlit limits of the night
Her white shell trembles amid crimson air,
And whilst the sleeping tempest gathers might,—

Doth, as the herald of its coming, bear
The ghost of its dead mother, whose dim form
Bends in dark ether from her infant's chair ;

So came a chariot on the silent storm
Of its own rushing splendour, and a Shape
So sate within, as one whom years deform,

Beneath a dusky hood and double cape,
Crouching within the shadow of a tomb.
And o'er what seemed the head a cloud-like crape

Was bent, a dun and faint ethereal gloom
Tempering the light.　Upon the chariot beam
A Janus-visaged Shadow did assume

The guidance of that wonder-wingèd team;
The shapes which drew it in thick lightnings
Were lost :—I heard alone on the air's soft stream

The music of their ever-moving wings.
All the four faces of that charioteer
Had their eyes banded; little profit brings

Speed in the van and blindness in the rear,
Nor then avail the beams that quench the sun,
Or that with banded eyes could pierce the sphere

Of all that is, has been, or will be done.
So ill was the car guided—but it past
With solemn speed majestically on.

The intense stirring of his imagination implied by this supreme poetic effort, the solitude of Villa Magni, and the elemental fervour of Italian heat to which he recklessly exposed himself, contributed to make Shelley more than usually nervous.　His somnambulism returned, and he saw visions.　On one occasion he thought that the dead Allegra rose from the sea, and clapped her hands, and laughed, and beckoned to him.　On another he roused the whole house at night by his screams, and remained terror-frozen in the trance produced by an appalling vision.　This mood he communicated, in some measure, to his friends.　One of them saw what she afterwards believed to have been his phantom, and another dreamed that he was dead.　They talked much of death, and it is noticeable that the

last words written to him by Jane were these :—" Are you
going to join your friend Plato ? "

The Leigh Hunts at last arrived in Genoa, whence they
again sailed for Leghorn.   Shelley heard the news upon
the 20th of June.   He immediately prepared to join them ;
and on the 1st of July set off with Williams in the
Don Juan, for Leghorn, where he rushed into the arms of
his old friend.   Leigh Hunt, in his autobiography, writes,
" I will not dwell upon the moment."   From Leghorn he
drove with the Hunts to Pisa, and established them in the
ground-floor of Byron's Palazzo Lanfranchi, as comfortably
as was consistent with his lordship's variable moods.   The
negotiations which had preceded Hunt's visit to Italy,
raised forebodings in Shelley's mind as to the reception he
would meet from Byron ; nor were these destined to be
unfulfilled.   Trelawny tells us how irksome the poet
found it to have " a man with a sick wife, and seven
disorderly children," established in his palace.   To Mrs.
Hunt he was positively brutal ; nor could he tolerate her
self-complacent husband, who, while he had voyaged far
and wide in literature, had never wholly cast the slough of
Cockneyism.   Hunt was himself hardly powerful enough
to understand the true magnitude of Shelley, though he
loved him ; and the tender solicitude of the great,
unselfish Shelley, for the smaller, harmlessly con-
ceited Hunt, is pathetic.   They spent a pleasant day
or two together, Shelley showing the Campo Santo and
other sights of Pisa to his English friend.   Hunt thought
him somewhat less hopeful than he used to be, but improved in health and strength and spirits.   One little
touch relating to their last conversation, deserves to be
recorded :— " He assented warmly to an opinion I expressed in the cathedral at Pisa, while the organ was

playing, that a truly divine religion might yet be established, if charity were really made the principle of it, instead of faith."

On the night following that day of rest, Shelley took a postchaise for Leghorn ; and early in the afternoon of the next day he set sail, with Williams, on his return voyage to Lerici. The sailor-boy, Charles Vivian, was their only companion. Trelawny, who was detained on board the *Bolivar*, in the Leghorn harbour, watched them start. The weather for some time had been unusually hot and dry. "Processions of priests and religiosi have been for several days past praying for rain ;" so runs the last entry in Williams's diary ; " but the gods are either angry or nature too powerful." Trelawny's Genoese mate observed, as the *Don Juan* stood out to sea, that they ought to have started at three a.m. instead of twelve hours later ; adding "the devil is brewing mischief." Then a sea-fog withdrew the *Don Juan* from their sight. It was an oppressively sultry afternoon. Trelawny went down into his cabin, and slept ; but was soon roused by the noise of the ships' crews in the harbour making all ready for a gale. In a short time the tempest was upon them, with wind, rain, and thunder. It did not last more than twenty minutes ; and at its end Trelawny looked out anxiously for Shelley's boat. She was nowhere to be seen, and nothing could be heard of her. In fact, though Trelawny could not then be absolutely sure of the catastrophe, she had sunk, struck in all probability by the prow of a felucca, but whether by accident or with the intention of running her down, is still uncertain.

On the morning of the third day after the storm, Trelawny rode to Pisa, and communicated his fears to Hunt. " I then went upstairs to Byron. When I told him, his lip

quivered, and his voice faltered as he questioned me."
Couriers were despatched to search the sea coast, and to bring
the *Bolivar* from Leghorn.   Trelawny rode in person toward
Via Reggio, and there found a punt, a water-keg, and some
bottles, which had been in Shelley's boat.   A week passed,
Trelawny patrolling the shore with the coast-guardsmen,
but hearing of no new discovery, until at last two bodies
were cast upon the sand.   One found near Via Reggio, on
the 18th of July, was Shelley's.   It had his jacket, "with
the volume of Æschylus in one pocket, and Keats's poems
in the other, doubled back, as if the reader, in the act of
reading, had hastily thrust it away."   The other, found
near the tower of Migliarino, at about four miles' distance,
was that of Williams.   The sailor-boy, Charles Vivian,
though cast up on the same day, the 18th of July, near
Massa, was not heard of by Trelawny till the 29th.

Nothing now remained but to tell the whole dreadful
truth to the two widowed women, who had spent the
last days in an agony of alternate despair and hope at
Villa Magni.   This duty Trelawny discharged faithfully
and firmly.   "The next day I prevailed on them," he
says, "to return with me to Pisa.   The misery of that
night and the journey of the next day, and of many
days and nights that followed, I can neither describe nor
forget."   It was decided that Shelley should be buried at
Rome, near his friend Keats and his son William, and
that Williams's remains should be taken to England.   But
first the bodies had to be burned; and for permission to
do this, Trelawny, who all through had taken the lead,
applied to the English Embassy at Florence.   After some
difficulty it was granted.

What remains to be said concerning the cremation of
Shelley's body on the 6th of August, must be told in

Trelawny's own words. Williams, it may be stated, had been burned on the preceding day.

" Three white wands had been stuck in the sand to mark the poet's grave, but as they were at some distance from each other, we had to cut a trench thirty yards in length, in the line of the sticks, to ascertain the exact spot, and it was nearly an hour before we came upon the grave.

" In the meantime Byron and Leigh Hunt arrived in the carriage, attended by soldiers, and the Health Officer, as before. The lonely and grand scenery that surrounded us, so exactly harmonized with Shelley's genius, that I could imagine his spirit soaring over us. The sea, with the islands of Gorgona, Capraja, and Elba, was before us ; old battlemented watch-towers stretched along the coast, backed by the marble-crested Apennines glistening in the sun, picturesque from their diversified outlines, and not a human dwelling was in sight.

" As I thought of the delight Shelley felt in such scenes of loneliness and grandeur whilst living, I felt we were no better than a herd of wolves or a pack of wild dogs, in tearing out his battered and naked body from the pure yellow sand that lay so lightly over it, to drag him back to the light of day ; but the dead have no voice, nor had I power to check the sacrilege—the work went on silently in the deep and unresisting sand, not a word was spoken, for the Italians have a touch of sentiment, and their feelings are easily excited into sympathy. Byron was silent and thoughtful. We were startled and drawn together by a dull, hollow sound that followed the blow of a mattock ; the iron had struck a skull, and the body was soon uncovered . . . . After the fire was well kindled we repeated the ceremony of the previous day ; and more

wine was poured over Shelley's dead body than he had
consumed during his life. This with the oil and salt
made the yellow flames glisten and quiver. The heat
from the sun and fire was so intense that the atmosphere
was tremulous and wavy . . . . The fire was so fierce as
to produce a white heat on the iron, and to reduce its
contents to grey ashes. The only portions that were not
consumed were some fragments of bones, the jaw, and the
skull ; but what surprised us all was that the heart remained entire. In snatching this relic from the fiery
furnace, my hand was severely burnt ; and had any one
seen me do the act, I should have been put into quaran-
tine."

Shelley's heart was given to Hunt, who subsequently,
not without reluctance and unseemly dispute, resigned it
to Mrs. Shelley. It is now at Boscombe. His ashes
were carried by Trelawny to Rome and buried in the
Protestant cemetery, so touchingly described by him in
his letter to Peacock, and afterwards so sublimely in
Adonais. The epitaph, composed by Hunt, ran thus :
"Percy. Bysshe Shelley, Cor Cordium, Natus iv. Aug.
MDCCXCII. Obiit VIII Jul. MDCCCXXII." To the Latin words
Trelawny, faithfullest and most devoted of friends, added
three lines from Ariel's song, much loved in life by
Shelley :

> Nothing of him that doth fade,
> But doth suffer a sea-change
> Into something rich and strange.

"And so," writes Lady Shelley, "the sea and the earth
closed over one who was great as a poet, and still greater
as a philanthropist ; and of whom it may be said, that
his wild spiritual character seems to have prepared him

for being thus snatched from life under circumstances of
mingled terror and beauty, while his powers were yet in
their spring freshness, and age had not come to render
the ethereal body decrepit, or to wither the heart which
could not be consumed by fire."

CHAPTER VIII.

AFTER some deliberation I decided to give this little work on Shelley the narrative rather than the essay form, impelled thereto by one commanding reason. Shelley's life and his poetry are indissolubly connected. He acted what he thought and felt, with a directness rare among his brethren of the poet's craft; while his verse, with the exception of *The Cenci,* expressed little but the animating thoughts and aspirations of his life. That life, moreover, was "a miracle of thirty years," so crowded with striking incident and varied experience that, as he said himself, he had already lived longer than his father and ought to be reckoned with the men of ninety. Through all vicissitudes he preserved his youth inviolate, and died, like one whom the gods love, or like a hero of Hellenic story, young, despite grey hairs and suffering. His life has, therefore, to be told, in order that his life-work may be rightly valued: for, great as that was, he, the man, was somehow greater; and noble as it truly is, the memory of himself is nobler.

To the world he presented the rare spectacle of a man passionate for truth, and unreservedly obedient to the right as he discerned it. The anomaly which made his practical career a failure, lay just here. The right he followed

was too often the antithesis of ordinary morality : in his
desire to cast away the false and grasp the true, he overshot the mark of prudence.   The blending in him of a
pure and earnest purpose with moral and social theories
that could not but have proved pernicious to mankind at
large, produced at times an almost grotesque mixture in
his actions no less than in his verse.   We cannot, therefore, wonder that society, while he lived, felt the necessity
of asserting itself against him.   But now that he has passed
into the company of the great dead, and time has softened
down the asperities of popular judgment, we are able to
learn the real lesson of his life and writings.   That is not
to be sought in any of his doctrines, but rather in his fearless bearing, his resolute loyalty to an unselfish and in the
simplest sense benevolent ideal.   It is this which consti-
tutes his supreme importance for us English at the present
time.   Ours is an age in which ideals are rare, and we
belong to a race in which men who follow them so single-
heartedly are not common.

As a poet, Shelley contributed a new quality to English
literature—a quality of ideality, freedom, and spiritual
audacity, which severe critics of other nations think we lack.
Byron's daring is in a different region : his elemental worldli-
ness and pungent satire do not liberate our energies, or cheer
us with new hopes and splendid vistas.   Wordsworth,
the very antithesis to Shelley in his reverent accord with
institutions, suits our meditative mood, sustains us with
a sound philosophy, and braces us by healthy contact
with the Nature he so dearly loved.   But in Wordsworth
there is none of Shelley's magnetism.   What remains of
permanent value in Coleridge's poetry—such work as
Christabel, the *Ancient Mariner*, or *Kubla Khan*—is a
product of pure artistic fancy, tempered by the author's

mysticism.   Keats, true and sacred poet as he was, loved
Nature with a somewhat sensuous devotion.   She was for
him a mistress rather than a Diotima; nor did he share
the prophetic fire which burns in Shelley's verse, quite
apart from the direct enunciation of his favourite tenets.   In
none of Shelley's greatest contemporaries was the lyrical
faculty so paramount; and whether we consider his minor
songs, his odes, or his more complicated choral dramas,
we acknowledge that he was the loftiest and the most
spontaneous singer of our language.   In range of power
he was also conspicuous above the rest.   Not only did
he write the best lyrics, but the best tragedy, the best
translations, and the best familiar poems of his century.
As a satirist and humourist, I cannot place him so high as
some of his admirers do; and the purely polemical
portions of his poems, those in which he puts forth his
antagonism to tyrants and religions and custom in all its
myriad forms, seem to me to degenerate at intervals
into poor rhetoric.

While his genius was so varied and its flight so un-
approached in swiftness, it would be vain to deny that
Shelley, as an artist, had faults from which the men with
whom I have compared him were more free.   The most prominent of these are haste, incoherence, verbal carelessness,
incompleteness, a want of narrative force, and a weak
hold on objective realities.   Even his warmest admirers,
if they are sincere critics, will concede that his verse, taken
altogether, is marked by inequality.   In his eager self-
abandonment to inspiration, he produced much that is
unsatisfying simply because it is not ripe.   There was no
defect of power in him, but a defect of patience; and
the final word to be pronounced in estimating the larger
bulk of his poetry is the word immature.   Not only

was the poet young; but the fruit of his young mind
had been plucked before it had been duly mellowed by
reflection. Again, he did not care enough for common
things to present them with artistic fulness. He was
intolerant of detail, and thus failed to model with the
roundness that we find in Goethe's work. He flew at
the grand, the spacious, the sublime; and did not always
succeed in realizing for his readers what he had imagined.
A certain want of faith in his own powers, fostered by
the extraordinary discouragement under which he had to
write, prevented him from finishing what he began, or
from giving that ultimate form of perfection to his longer
works which we admire in shorter pieces like the *Ode to
the West Wind*. When a poem was ready, he had it
hastily printed, and passed on to fresh creative efforts.
If anything occurred to interrupt his energy, he flung the
sketch aside. Some of these defects, if we may use this
word at all to indicate our sense that Shelley might by care
have been made equal to his highest self, were in a great
measure the correlative of his chief quality—the ideality,
of which I have already spoken. He composed with all
his faculties, mental, emotional, and physical, at the
utmost strain, at a white heat of intense fervour, striving
to attain one object, the truest and most passionate
investiture for the thoughts which had inflamed his ever-
quick imagination. The result is that his finest work
has more the stamp of something natural and elemental
—the wind, the sea, the depth of air—than of a mere
artistic product. Plato would have said: the Muses
filled this man with sacred madness, and, when he
wrote, he was no longer in his own control. There was,
moreover, ever-present in his nature an effort, an aspiration
after a better than the best this world can show

o

which prompted him to blend the choicest products of
his thought and fancy with the fairest images borrowed
from the earth on which he lived. He never willingly
composed except under the impulse to body forth a vision
of the love and light and life which was the spirit of the
power he worshipped. This persistent upward striving, this
earnestness, this passionate intensity, this piety of soul and
purity of inspiration, give a quite unique spirituality to his
poems. But it cannot be expected that the colder perfec-
tions of Academic art should be always found in them.
They have something of the waywardness and negligence
of nature, something of the *asymmetreia* we admire in
the earlier creations of Greek architecture. That Shelley,
acute critic and profound student as he was, could conform himself to rule and show himself an artist in the
stricter sense, is, however, abundantly proved by *The
Cenci* and by *Adonais.* The reason why he did not
always observe this method will be understood by those
who have studied his *Defence of Poetry,* and learned to
sympathize with his impassioned theory of art.

Working on this small scale, it is difficult to do
barest justice to Shelley's life or poetry. The materials
for the former are almost overwhelmingly copious and
strangely discordant. Those who ought to meet in love
over his grave, have spent their time in quarrelling about
him and baffling the most eager seeker for the truth.[1]
Through the turbid atmosphere of their recriminations it
is impossible to discern the whole personality of the man.
By careful comparison and refined manipulation of the
biographical treasures at our disposal, a fair portrait of

---

[1] See Lady Shelley *v.* Hogg; Trelawny *v.* the Shelley family;
Peacock *v.* Lady Shelley ; Garnett *v.* Peacock; Garnett *v.* Trelawny ; McCarthy *v.* Hogg, &c , &c.

Shelley might still be set before the reader with the
accuracy of a finished picture.   That labour of exquisite art
and of devoted love still remains to be accomplished, though
in the meantime Mr. W. M. Rossetti's Memoir is a most
valuable instalment.   Shelley in his lifetime bound those
who knew him with a chain of loyal affection, impressing
observers so essentially different as Hogg, Byron, Peacock,
Leigh Hunt, Trelawny, Medwin, Williams, with the conviction that he was the gentlest, purest, bravest, and most
spiritual being they had ever met.   The same conviction
is forced upon his biographer.   During his four last years
this most loveable of men was becoming gradually riper,
wiser, truer to his highest instincts.   The imperfections of
his youth were being rapidly absorbed.   His self-know-
ledge was expanding, his character mellowing, and his
genius growing daily stronger.   Without losing the fire
that burned in him, he had been lessoned by experience
into tempering its fervour ; and when he reached the age
of twenty-nine, he stood upon the height of his most
glorious achievement, ready to unfold his wings for a yet
sublimer flight.   At that moment, when life at last seemed
about to offer him rest, unimpeded activity, and happiness,
death robbed the world of his maturity.   Posterity has
but the product of his cruder years, the assurance that he
had already outlived them into something nobler, and the
tragedy of his untimely end.

If a final word were needed to utter the unutterable
sense of waste excited in us by Shelley's premature
absorption into the mystery of the unknown, we might
find it in the last lines of his own *Alastor:*—

> Art and eloquence,
> And all the shows o' the world, are frail and vain
> To weep a loss that turns their light to shade.

It is a woe "too deep for tears," when all
Is reft at once, when some surpassing spirit,
Whose light adorned the world around it, leaves
Those who remain behind nor sobs nor groans,
The passionate tumult of a clinging hope;
But pale despair and cold tranquillity,
Nature's vast frame, the web of human things,
Birth and the grave, that are not as they were.

THE END.

For EU product safety concerns, contact us at Calle de José Abascal, 56–1°, 28003 Madrid, Spain or eugpsr@cambridge.org.

www.ingramcontent.com/pod-product-compliance
Ingram Content Group UK Ltd.
Pitfield, Milton Keynes, MK11 3LW, UK
UKHW012345130625
459647UK00009B/535